THE TEMPEST

The RSC Shakespeare

Edited by Jonathan Bate and Eric Rasmussen

Chief Associate Editor: Héloïse Sénéchal

Associate Editors: Trey Jansen, Eleanor Lowe, Lucy Munro, Dee Anna Phares, Jan Sewell

The Tempest

Textual editing: Eric Rasmussen

Introduction and Shakespeare's Career in the Theatre: Jonathan Bate

Commentary: Héloïse Sénéchal and Charlotte Scott

Scene-by-Scene Analysis: Jan Sewell

In Performance: Karin Brown (RSC stagings) and Jan Sewell (overview)

The Director's Cut (interviews by Jonathan Bate and Kevin Wright): Peter Brook, Sam Mendes and Rupert Goold

Editorial Advisory Board

The RSC Shakespeare

WILLIAM SHAKESPEARE

THE TEMPEST

Edited by
Jonathan Bate and Eric Rasmussen

Introduced by Jonathan Bate

Macmillan

Published by arrangement with Modern Library, an imprint of The Random House Publishing Group, a division of Random House, Inc.

Published 2008 by
MACMILLAN PUBLISHERS LTD
Houndmills, Basingstoke, Hampshire RG21 6XS
Companies and representatives throughout the world

ISBN-13   978–0–230–21784–3 hardback
ISBN-13   978–0–230–21785–0 paperback

This book is printed on paper suitable for recycling and made from fully managed and sustained forest sources.

A catalogue record for this book is available from the British Library.

10   9   8   7   6   5   4   3   2
17   16   15   14   13   12

Printed in China

CONTENTS

INTRODUCTION

The Tempest was almost certainly Shakespeare's last solo-authored play. We do not, however, know whether he anticipated that this would be the case. It was also the first play to be printed in the First Folio of his collected works. Again, we do not know whether it was given pride of place because the editors of the Folio regarded it as a showpiece – the summation of the master's art – or for the more mundane reason that they had a clean copy in the clear hand of the scribe Ralph Crane, which would have given the compositors a relatively easy start as they set to work on the mammoth task of typesetting nearly a million words of Shakespeare. Whether it found its position by chance or design, *The Tempest*'s place at the end of Shakespeare's career and the beginning of his collected works has profoundly shaped responses to the play ever since the early nineteenth century. It has come to be regarded as the touchstone of Shakespearean interpretation.

Most of Shakespeare's plays have twenty or more scenes, at least as many roles, several different plot lines and a variety of imaginary locations. In some, the action takes place across a wide gap of time. In comparison, *The Tempest* is extremely simple: it only has nine scenes and a dozen speaking parts of substance. Miranda is the only female role, though Ariel would have provided a showcase for a boy-actor who could sing. After the short opening scene representing a ship struggling in a storm, all the remaining action takes place on Prospero's island. A series of very precise references to the timing of Ariel's release from his servitude suggests that the action takes place almost in 'real time', during a few hours on a single afternoon. For the first time since *The Comedy of Errors*, written nearly two decades earlier, Shakespeare conforms to the neo-classical 'unities', the idea that a well made play should have a single focus of time, place and action.

MASTERY AND RULE

The narrative is concentrated on questions of mastery and rule. During the tempest in the opening scene, the normal social order is out of joint: the boatswain commands the courtiers in the knowledge that the roaring waves care nothing for 'the name of king'. Then the back story, unfolded at length in Act 1 scene 2, tells of conspirators who do not respect the title of duke: we learn of Prospero's loss of power in Milan and the compensatory command he has gained over Ariel and Caliban on the island. The Ferdinand and Miranda love-knot is directed towards the future government of Milan and Naples. There is further politic plotting: Sebastian and Antonio's plan to murder King Alonso and good Gonzalo, the madcap scheme of the base-born characters to overthrow Prospero and make drunken butler Stephano king of the island. The theatrical coups performed by Prospero, assisted by Ariel and the other spirits of the island – the freezing of the conspirators, the harpy and the vanishing banquet, the masque of goddesses and agricultural workers, the revelation of the lovers playing at chess – all serve the purpose of requiting the sins of the past, restoring order in the present and preparing for a harmonious future. Once the work is done, Ariel is released (with a pang) and Prospero is ready to prepare his own spirit for death. Even Caliban will 'seek for grace'.

But Shakespeare never keeps it simple. Prospero's main aim in conjuring up the storm and bringing the court to the island is to force his usurping brother Antonio into repentance. Yet when the climactic confrontation comes, Antonio does not say a word in reply to Prospero's combination of forgiveness and demand ('I do forgive / Thy rankest fault – all of them – and require / My dukedom of thee, which perforce I know / Thou must restore'). He wholly fails to follow the good example set by Alonso a few lines before ('Thy dukedom I resign, and do entreat / Thou pardon me my wrongs'). As for Antonio's sidekick Sebastian, he has the temerity to ascribe Prospero's magical foresight to demonic influence ('The devil speaks in him'). For all the powers at Prospero's command, there is no way of predicting or controlling human nature. A conscience cannot be created where there is none.

By this time, Prospero has broken his staff. Ariel's key words in the speech that prompts the master to renounce his magic – his power – are 'were I human' (5.1.23). The fact that a non-human spirit has shown 'a touch, a feeling' for the afflictions of Prospero's enemies reveals to him that his own humanity requires him to forgive instead of revenge. The play is indeed an investigation of what it means to be human, or, to put it another way, of the meaning of humanism.

PROSPERO'S 'POTENT ART'

In Shakespeare's time, the essence of humanism was the idea of 'art'. To be human was to stand above the rest of nature by means of the arts of rational debate, eloquent speech and ethical responsibility. Humanism was above all an educational project that aimed to inculcate civic virtue: through reading and literary composition, through history, through the 'liberal arts', young men could be trained as public servants and loyal subjects. This is the main reason why there was a vigorous debate about the theatre in the period: the drama, with its ancient Greek and Roman precedents, had a venerable humanist pedigree, but the public stage was a less malleable arena than the university, and the theatre-going audience represented a more mixed and unruly clientele than the boys regimented in Elizabethan grammar schools. The fact that Prospero persistently uses theatre as an educational device suggests that *The Tempest* may be read as Shakespeare's interrogation of his own art.

Samuel Taylor Coleridge described Prospero as 'the very Shakespeare, as it were, of the tempest'. In other words, the leading character's conjuring up of the storm in the opening scene corresponds to the dramatist's conjuring up of the whole world of the play. The art of Prospero harnesses the power of nature in order to bring the other Italian characters to join him in his exile; by the same account, the art of Shakespeare transforms the platform of the stage into a ship at sea and then 'an uninhabited island'. 'If by your art, my dearest father,' says Miranda on Prospero's first appearance, 'you have / Put the wild waters in this roar, allay them.' A few lines later, he asks his daughter to help him take off his 'magic garment', which he addresses as 'my art'. 'Art' is thus established as the play's key word. Caliban is Prospero's 'other' because he represents the state of nature. In the Darwinian nineteenth century, he was recast as the 'missing link' between humankind and our animal ancestors.

Prospero then transforms the 'bare island' into a schoolroom. He delivers a series of history lessons to Miranda, to Ariel, to Caliban – and to the audience in the theatre. One senses that Miranda has been told the story of her life many times before and that on this occasion she is struggling to stay awake. As Duke of Milan, Prospero reminds her, he was 'for the liberal arts / Without a parallel'. Becoming more and more absorbed in his study, he delegated first the 'manage' (administration) and then the outright 'government' of his state to his brother Antonio. Prospero's mistake was to pursue learning for its own sake rather than as a means to a political end. In the sixteenth and seventeenth centuries, the 'liberal arts' were intended as tools for government, not distractions from it.

Prospero's name means 'fortunate', or more literally 'according to one's hopes'. This could also be a translation of the name of one of the most famous figures in the dramatic repertoire during Shakespeare's early years in the theatre: 'Faustus' is Latin for 'fortunate'. Marlowe's hugely successful play opened with a soliloquy in which Dr Faustus explains that he has become bored with the conventional curriculum of the liberal arts. He accordingly crosses the border into the dangerous territory of necromancy; he makes a pact with the devil, exchanging his immortal soul for the transitory power that magic can offer him; only when it is too late does he realize the error of his ways and cry out 'I'll burn my books'. Both the coincidence of name and Prospero's climactic line 'I'll drown my book', spoken as he abjures his 'rough magic', suggest that Shakespeare was courting parallels with *Dr Faustus*. The benign spirit Ariel and the 'deformed and savage slave' Caliban might be considered to serve an analogous function to the good and bad angels who watch over Faustus.

The difference from Marlowe is that Prospero claims to practise 'natural' as opposed to 'demonic' magic. Magical thinking was universal in the age of Shakespeare. Everyone was brought up to believe that there was another realm beyond that of nature, a realm of the spirit and of spirits. Natural and demonic magic were the two branches of the study and manipulation of preternatural phenomena. Magic meant the knowledge of hidden things and the art of working wonders. For some, it was the highest form of natural philosophy: the word came from *magia*, the ancient Persian term for wisdom. Sir Francis Bacon, in many ways a pioneer of scientific empiricism, did not hesitate to describe magic as 'a sublime wisdom, and the knowledge of the universal consents of things' (*De augmentis scientiarum*). The 'occult philosophy', as it was known, postulated a hierarchy of powers, with influence descending from disembodied ('intellectual') angelic spirits to the stellar and planetary world of the heavens to earthly things and their physical changes. The magician ascends to knowledge of higher powers and draws them down artificially to produce wonderful effects. Cornelius Agrippa, author of the influential *De occulta philosophia*, argued that 'ceremonial magic' was needed in order to reach the angelic intelligences above the stars. This was the highest and most dangerous level of activity, since it was all too easy – as Faustus found – to conjure up a devil instead of an angel. The more common form of 'natural magic' involved 'marrying' heaven to earth, working with the occult correspondences between the stars and the elements of the material world. The enduring conception of astrological influences is a vestige of this mode of thought. For a Renaissance mage such as Girolamo Cardano, who practised in Milan, medicine, natural philosophy, mathematics, astrology and dream interpretation were all intimately connected.

CALIBAN AND SYCORAX

Natural magic could never escape its demonic shadow. For every learned mage such as Agrippa or Cardano, there were a thousand village 'wise women' practising folk medicine and fortune-telling. All too often, the latter found themselves demonized as witches, blamed for crop failure, livestock disease and the other ills of life in the pre-modern era. Prospero is keen to contrast his own white magic with the black arts of Sycorax, Caliban's mother, but the play establishes strong parallels between them. He was exiled from Milan to the island because his devotion to his secret studies gave Antonio the opportunity to usurp the dukedom, while Sycorax was exiled from Algiers to the island because she was accused of witchcraft; he arrived with his young daughter, while she arrived pregnant with the child she had supposedly conceived by sleeping with the devil. Each of them can command the tides and manipulate the spirit-world that is embodied by Ariel. When Prospero comes to renounce his magic, he describes his powers in words borrowed from the incantation of another witch, Medea in Ovid's great storehouse of ancient mythological tales, the *Metamorphoses*. Thus Prospero: 'Ye elves of hills, brooks, standing lakes and groves ...', And Medea in Arthur Golding's Elizabethan translation of the *Metamorphoses*, one of Shakespeare's favourite books: 'Ye elves of hills, of brooks, of woods alone, / Of standing lakes, and of the night ...'.

Prospero at some level registers his own kinship with Sycorax when he says of Caliban 'this thing of darkness I / Acknowledge mine'. The splitting of subject and verb across the line ending here, ensuring a moment's hesitation in the acknowledgement, is an extreme instance of the suppleness with which late Shakespeare handles his iambic pentameter verse.

Shakespeare loved to set up oppositions, then shade his black and white into grey areas of moral complexity. In Milan, Prospero's inward-looking study of the liberal arts had led to the loss of power and the establishment of tyranny. On the island he seeks to make amends by applying what he has learned, by using active magic to bring repentance, restore his dukedom and set up a dynastic marriage. Yet at the beginning of the fifth act he sees that to be truly human is a matter not of exercising wisdom for the purposes of rule, but of practising a more strictly Christian version of virtue. For humanism, education in princely virtue meant the cultivation for political ends of wisdom, magnanimity, temperance and integrity. For Prospero what finally matters is kindness. And this is something that the master learns from his pupil: it is Ariel who teaches Prospero about 'feeling', not vice versa.

Ariel represents fire and air, concord and music, loyal service. Caliban is of the earth, associated with discord, drunkenness and rebellion. Ariel's medium of expression is delicate verse, while Caliban's is for the most part a robust, often ribald prose like that of the jester Trinculo and drunken butler Stephano. But, astonishingly, it is Caliban who speaks the play's most beautiful verse when he hears the music of Ariel: 'Be not afeard, the isle is full of noises, / Sounds and sweet airs that give delight and hurt not ...'. Even in prose, Caliban has a wonderful attunement to the natural environment: he knows every corner, every species of the island. Prospero calls him 'A devil, a born devil, on whose nature / Nurture can never stick', yet in the very next speech Caliban enters with the line 'Pray you, tread softly, that the blind mole may not hear a footfall', words of such strong imagination that Prospero's claim is instantly belied.

Caliban's purported sexual assault on Miranda shows that Prospero failed in his attempt to tame the animal instincts of the 'man-monster' and educate him into humanity. But who bears responsibility for the failure? Could it be that the problem arises from what Prospero has imprinted on Caliban's memory, not from the latter's nature? Caliban initially welcomed Prospero to the island and offered to share its fruits, every bit in the manner of the 'noble savages' in Michel de Montaigne's essay 'Of the Cannibals', which was another source from which Shakespeare quoted in the play (Gonzalo's Utopian 'golden age' vision of how he would govern the isle is borrowed from the English translation of Montaigne). Caliban only acts basely after Prospero has printed that baseness on him; what makes Caliban 'filth' may be the lessons in which Prospero has taught him that he is 'filth'. According to humanist theory, the learning of language is what makes man god-like as opposed to beast-like, but Caliban's only profit from the language lessons delivered to him by Prospero and Miranda is the ability to curse.

Caliban understands the power of the book: as fashioners of modern *coups d'état* begin by seizing the television station, so he stresses that the rebellion against Prospero must begin by taking possession of his books. But Stephano has another book. 'Here is that which will give language to you', he says to Caliban, replicating Prospero's gaining of control through language – but in a different mode. Textual inculcation is replaced by intoxication: the book that is kissed is the bottle. The dialogic spirit that is fostered by Shakespeare's technique of scenic counterpoint thus calls into question Prospero's use of books. If Stephano and Trinculo achieve through their alcohol what Prospero achieves through his teaching (in each case Caliban is persuaded to serve and to share the fruits of the isle), is not that teaching exposed as potentially nothing more than a means of social control? Prospero often seems more interested in the power-structure that is established by his schoolmastering than in the substance of what he teaches. It is hard to see how making Ferdinand carry logs is intended to inculcate virtue; its purpose is to elicit submission.

PLANTATION AND THE BRAVE NEW WORLD

Arrival on an island uninhabited by Europeans, talk of 'plantation', an encounter with a 'savage' in which alcohol is exchanged for survival skills, a process of language learning in which it is made clear who is master and who is slave, fear that the slave will impregnate the master's daughter, the desire to make the savage seek for Christian 'grace' (though also a proposal that he should be shipped to England and exhibited for profit), references to the dangerous weather of the Bermudas and to a 'brave new world': in all these respects, *The Tempest* conjures up the spirit of European colonialism. Shakespeare had contacts with members of the Virginia Company, which had been established by royal charter in 1606 and was instrumental in the foundation of the Jamestown colony in America the following year. Sometime in the autumn of 1610, a letter reached England describing how a fleet sent to reinforce the colony had been broken up by a storm in the Caribbean; the ship carrying the new governor had been driven to Bermuda, where the crew and passengers had wintered. Though the letter was not published at the time, it circulated in manuscript and inspired at least two pamphlets about these events. Scholars debate the extent to which Shakespeare made direct use of these materials, but certain details of the storm and the island seem to be derived from them. There is no doubt that the seemingly miraculous survival of the governor's party and the fertile environment they discovered in the Bahamas were topics of great public interest at the time of the play.

The British Empire, the slave trade and the riches of the spice routes lay in the future. Shakespeare's play is set in the Mediterranean, not the Caribbean. Caliban cannot strictly be described as a native of the island. And yet the play intuits the dynamic of colonial possession and dispossession with such uncanny power that in 1950 a book by Octave Mannoni called *The Psychology of Colonisation* could argue that the process functioned by means of a pair of reciprocal neuroses: the 'Prospero complex' on the part of the colonizer and the 'Caliban complex' on that of the colonized. It was in response to Mannoni that Frantz Fanon wrote *Black Skin, White Masks*, a book that did much to shape the intellectual terrain of the 'post-colonial' era. For many Anglophone Caribbean writers of the late twentieth century, *The Tempest*, and the figure of Caliban in particular, became a focal point for discovery of their own literary voices. The play is less a reflection of imperial history – after all, Prospero is an exile, not a venturer – than an anticipation of it.

In terms of real political power, the British Empire at the time of the play extended no further than Ireland. That island of colonial 'plantations' and supposedly savage yet poetic natives may lie in the hinterland of Shakespeare's imagination, but the main political emphasis of the play is court intrigue rather than imperial endeavour. As in so much drama of the age, Italy – the land of courtly sophistication and cunning, of Castiglione and Machiavelli – serves as backdrop. Italy did not become a unified nation until the nineteenth century. In Shakespeare's time, it was dominated by five separate city-states: Milan, Venice, Florence, Naples and Rome. Each was marked by rivalry with the others, internal factional division, and external pressures from Spain, France and the Holy Roman Empire. By setting their plays amid the Italian maelstrom of the earlier sixteenth century, Shakespeare and his contemporaries could engage in theatrical debate about monarchy and republicanism, idealism and realpolitik, dynastic liaison and internecine strife, without offending the Master of the Revels who cast an austere censor's eye over every play script with a view to the suppression of any contentious matter concerning Elizabethan and Jacobean politics and religious controversy.

COURT AND MASQUE

The first recorded performance of *The Tempest* took place on the evening of All Saints' Day, 1 November 1611, in the presence of King James at Whitehall. Just over a year later, in February 1613, the play was one of fourteen performed by Shakespeare's company, the King's Men, as their contribution to court celebrations marking the marriage of the king's daughter Elizabeth to Prince Frederick, Count Palatine and later King of Bohemia. It has sometimes been supposed that the wedding masque staged by Prospero's spirits for Miranda and Ferdinand was an addition to the script especially for this occasion, but there is no evidence for this supposition. *The Tempest* is no more and no less a courtly play than any of Shakespeare's other dramas. It was not commissioned for any particular court occasion, but – like all the other plays written for the King's Men – it was created in the knowledge that it would at some time be played at court.

Given his theatre company's status as the king's own players, Shakespeare remained politically guarded but made it his business to show an interest in the things that the king was interested in, such as witchcraft (*Macbeth*) and the question of the number of kingdoms into which Britain should be divided (*King Lear*). In the years when he was writing his last plays, the king and his courtiers were much preoccupied with royal marriages and the potential of dynastic liaisons to heal Europe's divisions. King James of Scotland and England was in the unique position of sitting on two Protestant thrones, while being the son of a famous Roman Catholic (Mary Queen of Scots). His wife, Anne of Denmark, had Catholic sympathies. He was therefore well qualified for his chosen role as an international peacemaker: the marriage of his son to a Catholic princess from Spain and his daughter to a Protestant prince from the Germanic territories would have been a strong strategic move. Though Shakespeare rigorously eschewed topicality and did not take the risk of seeking to advise his monarch on matters of policy, *The Tempest* is very much a drama of the moment: the duchy of Milan and the kingdom of Naples, together with the rivalry and intrigue of their rulers, stand as shorthand for the fractured polity of Europe, while the union of Miranda and Ferdinand embodies the hope that royal marriage might bring peace and stability. The game of chess was a powerful symbol for skilful statecraft and diplomatic manoeuvring. Miranda and Ferdinand's banter over their chess-board has typically Shakespearean equipoise: does the accusation of cheating suggest the fragility of the alliance between Milan and Naples or does the good humour of the exchange suggest that Italy will be in safe hands?

As regular players in the Whitehall Palace, the King's Men knew that from the end of 1608 onwards, the teenage Princess Elizabeth was resident at court. A cultured young woman who enjoyed music and dancing, she participated in court festivals and in 1610 danced in a masque called *Tethys*. Masques – performed by a mixed cast of royalty, courtiers and professional actors, staged with spectacular scenery and elaborate music – were the height of fashion at court in these years. Shakespeare's friend and rival Ben Jonson, working in conjunction with the designer Inigo Jones, was carving out a role for himself as the age's leading masque-wright. In 1608 he introduced the 'antimasque' (or 'antemasque'), a convention whereby grotesque figures known as 'antics' danced boisterously prior to the graceful and harmonious masque itself. Shakespeare nods to contemporary fashion by including a betrothal masque within the action of *The Tempest*, together with the antimasque farce of Caliban, Stephano and Trinculo smelling of horse-piss, stealing clothes from a line and being chased away by dogs. One almost wonders whether the figure of Prospero is a gentle parody of Ben Jonson: his theatrical imagination is bound by the classical unities (as Jonson's was) and he stages a court masque (as Jonson did). Perhaps this is why a few years later, in his *Bartholomew Fair*, Jonson parodied *The Tempest* in return.

The masque also provides the occasion for Shakespeare to continue his meditation upon the power of 'art'. Sometime schoolmaster Prospero has turned himself into a theatrical impresario. Having first staged the harpy's banquet, now he educates Ferdinand and Miranda into virtue (which in their case he makes synonymous with chastity) through dramatic spectacle. The hope here is that theatre can do what humanism traditionally relied on books to do. But – as is the way with live theatre – things do not go quite according to plan: to Prospero's irritation, the performance is interrupted by the entrance of Caliban and company.

POETIC FAITH

The play moves towards forgiveness, but also renunciation. The book of art is drowned. The masque and its players dissolve into vacancy:

> ... These our actors,
> As I foretold you, were all spirits and
> Are melted into air, into thin air,
> And, like the baseless fabric of this vision,
> The cloud-capped towers, the gorgeous palaces,
> The solemn temples, the great globe itself,
> Yea, all which it inherit, shall dissolve,
> And, like this insubstantial pageant faded,
> Leave not a rack behind. We are such stuff
> As dreams are made on; and our little life
> Is rounded with a sleep. ...

What endures is the power of the poetry. This passage, especially its last sentence, has become one of the great Shakespearean quotations: it is the kind of passage that a Renaissance reader, scanning a book for 'sentences' of deep wisdom about life, would have underlined or marked in the margin.

Stylistically, the speech is typical of the fluid verse of late Shakespeare. Crudely speaking, early Shakespearean verse is characterized by a preponderance of end-stopped verse lines, frequent use of rhyme and a wide array of highly visible rhetorical figures – repetitions, variations, balanced pairs – that impart shape and symmetry to the poetry, assisting the actor in remembering his part and the spectator in perceiving the play's language as memorable. Late Shakespearean verse, by contrast, is more flexible. There is a preponderance of run-on or enjambed lines, thoughts that spill over the line-ending and set up a tension between the movement of the metre and that of the grammar. The metre itself is also more varied: although the five beats of the iambic pentameter remain the underlying pulse or heartbeat, the rhythm measured to match the breath and pitch of English speech, irregularities are frequent. Subject and verb may be split across the line-ending. Half-lines, incomplete lines, feminine endings (an extra offbeat syllable), bold variations in the position of the caesura or mid-line pause, elaborations of simile and metaphor that snake across a whole speech: such arts serve to create the illusion of a character thinking in the moment and turning the thought to words, as opposed to an actor reciting a rhetorically finished prepared speech.

Thus: 'These our actors' (sentence beginning in the middle of a verse line), pause, 'As I foretold you' (parenthetic reference back to earlier dialogue), pause, 'were all spirits and' (verse line ends with a forward-thrusting 'and' instead of the customary pausal punctuation mark) 'Are melted into air', pause for elaboration, 'into thin air', take breath before launching into elaborated simile, then the towers, the palaces, the temples, the globe (each with its adjective and for the globe a special gesture or intonation in recognition that the theatre-home of 'these our actors' was 'the great Globe itself'), pause again, to gather and strengthen the strands of the thought with 'Yea', then through an asymmetrical parallelism of short and long, little function words and large-meaning verbs ('all which it' played off against 'shall' and 'inherit' against 'dissolve'), then a repetition of the structure established four lines before ('And, like'), but with an upping of the ante ('baseless fabric' inflated to 'insubstantial pageant'), and finally fade after 'faded' to the completion of the sentence in the half-line 'Leave not a rack behind', the key word being 'rack', which primarily means a wisp of cloud, thus clinching the sustained comparison of actors, theatre and life itself to *weather* –

English weather, evanescent, always changeable – but also, by means of the play on 'wreck' (which in Shakespearean English was pronounced and sometimes spelled 'wrack'), evoking the particular form of extreme weather, namely tempest, that Prospero has conjured up at the beginning of the play. The subtlety of the verse movement matches the complexity of the thought. Through the vocal art of a skilled actor, the 'beating mind' and the beats of the verse are as one.

Prospero's renunciations suggest that the play itself is profoundly sceptical of the power of the book and even of the theatre. The closing sections of the dialogue focus on traditional religious themes such as the search for grace and the preparation of the soul for death. Prospero's Christian language reaches its most sustained pitch in the epilogue, but his final request is for the indulgence not of God but of the audience. At the last moment, humanist learning is replaced not by Christian but by theatrical faith. Because of this it has been possible for the play to be read, as it so often has been since the Romantic period, as a credo, an *apologia pro vita sua* (a justification of his own life), on the part of Shakespeare the dramatist. The drama's own afterlife folds back its interior movement from secular to sacred: *The Tempest* has become a work of secular scripture. When art took over some of the functions of religion in the nineteenth and twentieth centuries, as Matthew Arnold predicted it would, Shakespeare became a kind of God, and the role which *The Tempest* performed became analogous to that which classical texts such as Virgil's *Aeneid* performed for humanism. Humanism became the humanities and Shakespeare became the classic text at the centre of the literary curriculum, where he still remains. This edition feeds that process, but with its particular emphasis on the play in performance – explored in the essays on Shakespeare's career in the theatre and on the play's stage history, and above all through the inclusion of the voices of distinguished directors – it also seeks to return *The Tempest* to the theatre.

Selections from critical commentaries on the play, with linking narrative, are available on the edition website, www.rscshakespeare.co.uk.

ABOUT THE TEXT

Shakespeare endures through history. He illuminates later times as well as his own. He helps us to understand the human condition. But he cannot do this without a good text of the plays. Without editions there would be no Shakespeare. That is why every twenty years or so throughout the last three centuries there has been a major new edition of his complete works. One aspect of editing is the process of keeping the texts up to date – modernizing the spelling, punctuation and typography (though not, of course, the actual words), providing explanatory notes in the light of changing educational practices (a generation ago, most of Shakespeare's classical and biblical allusions could be assumed to be generally understood, but now they can't).

But because Shakespeare did not personally oversee the publication of his plays, with some plays there are major editorial difficulties. Decisions have to be made as to the relative authority of the early printed editions, the pocket format 'Quartos' published in Shakespeare's lifetime and the elaborately produced 'First Folio' text of 1623, the original 'Complete Works' prepared for the press after his death by Shakespeare's fellow-actors, the people who knew the plays better than anyone else. *The Tempest*, however, exists only in a Folio text that is extremely well printed. Save for a handful of possible misprints, the Folio is highly trustworthy and unusually easy to edit.

The following notes highlight various aspects of the editorial process and indicate conventions used in the text of this edition:

Lists of Parts are supplied in the First Folio for only six plays, of which *The Tempest* is one. Capitals indicate that part of the name which is used for speech headings in the script (thus 'PROSPERO, the right Duke of Milan').

Locations are provided by the Folio for only two plays, of which *The Tempest*, set on 'an uninhabited Island', is one. Eighteenth-century editors, working in an age of elaborately realistic stage sets, were the first to provide detailed locations ('another part of the island'). Given that Shakespeare wrote for a bare stage and often an imprecise sense of place, we have relegated locations to the explanatory notes at the foot of the page, where they are given at the beginning of each scene where the imaginary location is different from the one before. We have emphasized broad geographical settings rather than specifics of the kind that suggest anachronistically realistic staging.

Act and Scene Divisions were provided in the Folio in a much more thoroughgoing way than in the Quartos. Sometimes, however, they were erroneous or omitted; corrections and additions supplied by editorial tradition are indicated by square brackets. Five-act division is based on a classical model, and act breaks provided the opportunity to replace the candles in the indoor Blackfriars playhouse which the King's Men used after 1608, but Shakespeare did not necessarily think in terms of a five-part structure of dramatic composition. The Folio convention is that a scene ends when the stage is empty. Nowadays, partly under the influence of film, we tend to consider a scene to be a dramatic unit that ends with either a change of imaginary location or a significant passage of time within the narrative. Shakespeare's fluidity of composition accords well with this convention, so in addition to act and scene numbers we provide a *running scene* count in the right margin at the beginning of each new scene, in the typeface used for editorial directions. Where there is a scene break caused by a momentary bare stage, but the location does not change and extra time does not pass, we use the convention *running scene continues*. There is inevitably a degree of editorial judgement in making such calls, but the system is very valuable in suggesting the pace of the plays.

Speakers' Names are often inconsistent in Folio. We have regularized speech headings, but retained an element of deliberate inconsistency in entry directions, in order to give the flavour of Folio.

Verse is indicated by lines that do not run to the right margin and by capitalization of each line. The Folio printers sometimes set verse as prose, and vice versa (either out of misunderstanding or for reasons of space). We have silently corrected in such cases, although in some instances there is ambiguity, in which case we have leaned towards the preservation of Folio layout. Folio sometimes uses contraction ('turnd' rather than 'turned') to indicate whether or not the final '-ed' of a past participle is sounded, an area where there is variation for the sake of the five-beat iambic pentameter rhythm. We use the convention of a grave accent to indicate sounding (thus 'turnèd' would be two syllables), but would urge actors not to overstress. In cases where one speaker ends with a verse half-line and the next begins with the other half of the pentameter, editors since the late eighteenth century have indented the second line. We have abandoned this convention, since the Folio does not use it, and nor did actors' cues in the Shakespearean theatre. An exception is made when the second speaker actively interrupts or completes the first speaker's sentence.

Spelling is modernized, but older forms are very occasionally maintained where necessary for rhythm or aural effect.

Punctuation in Shakespeare's time was as much rhetorical as grammatical. 'Colon' was originally a term for a unit of thought in an argument. The semi-colon was a new unit of punctuation (some of the Quartos lack them altogether). We have modernized punctuation throughout, but have given more weight to Folio punctuation than many editors, since, though not Shakespearean, it reflects the usage of his period. In particular, we have used the colon far more than many editors: it is exceptionally useful as a way of indicating how many Shakespearean speeches unfold clause by clause in a developing argument that gives the illusion of enacting the process of thinking in the moment. We have also kept in mind the origin of punctuation in classical times as a way of assisting the actor and orator: the comma suggests the briefest of pauses for breath, the colon a middling one and a full stop or period a longer pause. Semi-colons, by contrast, belong to an era of punctuation that was only just coming in during Shakespeare's time and that is coming to an end now: we have accordingly only used them where they occur in our copy-texts (and not always then). Dashes are sometimes used for parenthetical interjections where the Folio has brackets. They are also used for interruptions and changes in train of thought. Where a change of addressee occurs within a speech, we have used a dash preceded by a full stop (or occasionally another form of punctuation). Often the identity of the respective addressees is obvious from the context. When it is not, this has been indicated in a marginal stage direction.

Entrances and Exits are fairly thorough in Folio, which has accordingly been followed as faithfully as possible. Where characters are omitted or corrections are necessary, this is indicated by square brackets (e.g. '[*and Attendants*]'). *Exit* is sometimes silently normalized to *Exeunt* and *Manet* anglicized to 'remains'. We trust Folio positioning of entrances and exits to a greater degree than most editors.

Editorial Stage Directions such as stage business, asides, indications of addressee and of characters' position on the gallery stage are only used sparingly in Folio. Other editions mingle directions of this kind with original Folio and Quarto directions, sometimes marking them by means of square brackets. We have sought to distinguish what could be described as *directorial* interventions of this kind from Folio-style directions (either original or supplied) by placing them in the right margin in a different typeface. There is a degree of subjectivity about which directions are of which kind, but the procedure is intended as a reminder to the reader and the actor that Shakespearean stage directions are often dependent upon editorial inference alone and are not set in stone. We also depart from editorial tradition in sometimes admitting uncertainty and thus printing permissive stage directions, such as an *Aside?* (often a line may be equally effective as an aside or a direct address — it is for each production or reading to make its own decision) or a *may exit* or a piece of business placed between arrows to indicate that it may occur at various different moments within a scene.

Line Numbers in the left margin are editorial, for reference and to key the explanatory and textual notes.

Explanatory Notes at the foot of each page explain allusions and gloss obsolete and difficult words, confusing phraseology, occasional major textual cruces, and so on. Particular attention is given to non-standard usage, bawdy innuendo and technical terms (e.g. legal and military language). Where more than one sense is given, commas indicate shades of related meaning, slashes alternative or double meanings.

Textual Notes at the end of the play indicate major departures from the Folio. They take the following form: the reading of our text is given in bold and its source given after an equals sign, with 'F2' indicating that it derives from the Second Folio of 1632 and 'Ed' that it derives from the subsequent editorial tradition. The rejected Folio ('F') reading is then given. Thus for Act 4 scene 1 line 57: '**4.1.57 abstemious** = F2. F = abstenious'. This means that the Folio compositor erroneously printed the word 'abstenious' and the Second Folio corrected it to 'abstemious'.

KEY FACTS

MAJOR PARTS: (*with percentage of lines/number of speeches/scenes on stage*) Prospero (30%/115/5), Ariel (9%/45/6), Caliban (8%/50/5), Stephano (7%/60/4), Gonzalo (7%/52/4), Sebastian (5%/67/4), Antonio (6%/57/4), Miranda (6%/49/4), Ferdinand (6%/31/4), Alonso (5%/40/4), Trinculo (4%/39/4).

LINGUISTIC MEDIUM: 80% verse, 20% prose.

DATE: 1611. Performed at court, 1 November 1611; uses source material not available before autumn 1610.

SOURCES: No known source for main plot, but some details of the tempest and the island seem to derive from William Strachey, *A True Reportory of the Wreck and Redemption of Sir Thomas Gates, Knight* (written 1610, published in *Purchas his Pilgrims*, 1625) and perhaps Sylvester Jourdain, *A Discovery of the Bermudas* (1610) and the Virginia Company's pamphlet *A True Declaration of the Estate of the Colony in Virginia* (1610); several allusions to Virgil's *Aeneid* and Ovid's *Metamorphoses* (most notably the imitation in Act 5 scene 1 of Arthur Golding's 1567 translation of Medea's incantation in Ovid's 7th book); Gonzalo's 'golden age' oration in Act 2 scene 1 based closely on Michel de Montaigne's essay 'Of the Cannibals', translated by John Florio (1603).

TEXT: First Folio of 1623 is the only early printed text. Based on a transcript by Ralph Crane, professional scribe working for the King's Men. Generally good quality of printing.

THE TEMPEST

PROSPERO, the right Duke of Milan

MIRANDA, his daughter

ALONSO, King of Naples

SEBASTIAN, his brother

ANTONIO, Prospero's brother, the usurping Duke of Milan

FERDINAND, son to the King of Naples

GONZALO, an honest old councillor

ADRIAN and **FRANCISCO**, lords

TRINCULO, a jester

STEPHANO, a drunken butler

MASTER of a ship

BOATSWAIN

MARINERS

CALIBAN, a savage and deformed slave

ARIEL, an airy spirit

Spirits commanded by Prospero playing roles of } **IRIS** **CERES** **JUNO** **NYMPHS** **REAPERS**

The Scene: an uninhabited island

Act 1 Scene 1   *running scene 1*

*A tempestuous noise of thunder and lightning heard. Enter a
Shipmaster and a Boatswain*

MASTER Boatswain!

BOATSWAIN Here, master. What cheer?

MASTER Good: speak to th'mariners. Fall to't yarely, or
we run ourselves aground! Bestir, bestir!   *Exit*
Enter Mariners

5   **BOATSWAIN** Heigh, my hearts! Cheerly, cheerly, my
hearts! Yare, yare! Take in the topsail. Tend to
th'master's whistle.— Blow, till thou burst thy wind,   *To the storm*
if room enough.

*Enter Alonso, Sebastian, Antonio, Ferdinand, Gonzalo and
others*

ALONSO Good boatswain, have care. Where's the
10   master? Play the men.

BOATSWAIN I pray now, keep below.

ANTONIO Where is the master, boatswain?

BOATSWAIN Do you not hear him? You mar our labour.
Keep your cabins! You do assist the storm.

15   **GONZALO** Nay, good, be patient.

BOATSWAIN When the sea is. Hence! What cares these
roarers for the name of king? To cabin! Silence!
Trouble us not.

GONZALO Good, yet remember whom thou hast aboard.

20   **BOATSWAIN** None that I more love than myself. You are
a counsellor: if you can command these elements to
silence, and work the peace of the present, we will
not hand a rope more: use your authority. If you
cannot, give thanks you have lived so long, and

25   make yourself ready in your cabin for the mischance
of the hour, if it so hap.— Cheerly, good hearts!—   *To the Mariners*
Out of our way, I say.   *To the Courtiers*

*Exeunt [Boatswain with Mariners, followed by Alonso,
Sebastian, Antonio and Ferdinand]*

1.1 *Location: a ship at sea* **Boatswain** ship's chief officer   **2 cheer** news/encouragement   **3 Good** good
fellow/good, you're there   **yarely** swiftly   **4 Bestir** be active   **5 hearts** hearties   **Cheerly** heartily, willingly
6 Yare quick   **Take … topsail** reducing the sail lessens the force of the wind pushing the ship toward
land   **Tend** pay attention   **7 Blow … enough** blow until you burst, as long as we have enough rock-free
sea to manoeuvre in   **9 have** take   **10 Play the** act like   **13 mar** ruin   **16 Hence!** Be gone!   **17 roarers**
waves/riotous people   **21 counsellor** adviser/member of the king's council   **22 work … present** calm the
current events   **23 hand** handle   **26 hap** happen

GONZALO I have great comfort from this fellow:
methinks he hath no drowning mark upon him: his
30   complexion is perfect gallows. Stand fast, good Fate,
to his hanging: make the rope of his destiny our
cable, for our own doth little advantage. If he be not
born to be hanged, our case is miserable.   *Exit*
Enter Boatswain
BOATSWAIN Down with the topmast! Yare! Lower, lower!
35   Bring her to try with main course. (*A cry within*) A
plague upon this howling! They are louder than the
weather or our office.
Enter Sebastian, Antonio and Gonzalo
Yet again? What do you here? Shall we give o'er and
drown? Have you a mind to sink?
40   SEBASTIAN A pox o'your throat, you bawling,
blasphemous, incharitable dog!
BOATSWAIN Work you then.
ANTONIO Hang, cur! Hang, you whoreson, insolent
noisemaker! We are less afraid to be drowned than
45   thou art.
GONZALO I'll warrant him for drowning, though the ship
were no stronger than a nutshell and as leaky as an
unstanched wench.
BOATSWAIN Lay her ahold, ahold! Set her two courses off
50   to sea again! Lay her off!
Enter Mariners, wet
MARINERS All lost! To prayers, to prayers! All lost!
BOATSWAIN What, must our mouths be cold?
GONZALO The king and prince at prayers: let's assist
them, for our case is as theirs.
55   SEBASTIAN I'm out of patience.
ANTONIO We are merely cheated of our lives by
drunkards. This wide-chopped rascal: would thou
mightst lie drowning, the washing of ten tides!

29 he … gallows 'he that is born to be hanged shall never be drowned' (proverbial) **mark** ominous indicator **31 rope … destiny** i.e. the hangman's noose **32 cable** anchor rope **34 Down … topmast!** reduce the height of the ship's main mast (to increase stability) **35 to … course** i.e. as near as possible to a standstill **37 our office** we are as we undertake our work **38 o'er** up **40 pox** plague **43 cur** dog **46 warrant … drowning** guarantee he will not drown **48 unstanched** promiscuous/sexually unsatisfied/menstruating freely **49 Lay her ahold** keep the ship steady by sailing close to the wind **Set … sea** raise both fore-sail and main-sail in order to drive the ship into open sea **52 must … cold** i.e. must we die/must our prayers be ineffective **56 merely** completely **57 wide-chopped** loud-mouthed/with mouth wide open **58 ten tides** pirates were hanged on the shore where their bodies remained during three tides

GONZALO He'll be hanged yet,
60   Though every drop of water swear against it
        And gape at wid'st to glut him.

                            [*Exeunt Boatswain and Mariners*]

A confused noise within

[VOICES OFF-STAGE]   Mercy on us! — We split, we split!
        — Farewell, my wife and children! — Farewell,
        brother! — We split, we split, we split!
65   ANTONIO Let's all sink wi'th'king.
     SEBASTIAN Let's take leave of him.

                            Exeunt [*Antonio and Sebastian*]

     GONZALO Now would I give a thousand furlongs of sea
        for an acre of barren ground: long heath, brown
        furze, anything. The wills above be done! But I would
70   fain die a dry death.   *Exit*

Act 1 Scene 2   *running scene 2*

Enter Prospero and Miranda

     MIRANDA If by your art, my dearest father, you have
        Put the wild waters in this roar, allay them.
        The sky, it seems, would pour down stinking pitch,
        But that the sea, mounting to th'welkin's cheek,
5   Dashes the fire out. O, I have suffered
        With those that I saw suffer: a brave vessel —
        Who had, no doubt, some noble creature in her —
        Dashed all to pieces. O, the cry did knock
        Against my very heart. Poor souls, they perished.
10   Had I been any god of power, I would
        Have sunk the sea within the earth, or ere
        It should the good ship so have swallowed, and
        The fraughting souls within her.
     PROSPERO Be collected:
15   No more amazement. Tell your piteous heart
        There's no harm done.
     MIRANDA O, woe the day!

---

59 **hanged yet** i.e. will survive to be hanged on land   61 **at wid'st** wide open   **glut** swallow   62 **We split** the ship is splitting apart/we are shipwrecked   67 **furlong** 220 yards   68 **acre** furlong   **long heath** heather   **brown furze** withered gorse   70 **fain** rather   1.2 *Location: the rest of the play is set in various parts of Prospero's island*   ***Prospero*** from Latin for 'to cause to succeed'; in Italian and Spanish means 'fortunate, prosperous'   ***Miranda*** from Latin for 'to wonder, marvel'; means 'she who is admired'   1 **art** skill, magic, learning   2 **allay** calm   3 **pitch** black substance obtained from boiling tar   4 **th'welkin's** the sky's   5 **fire** lightning   6 **brave** splendid   11 **or ere** before   13 **fraughting souls** those constituting the freight (cargo)   14 **collected** calm, composed   15 **amazement** fear/wonder

PROSPERO No harm:
    I have done nothing but in care of thee —
20   Of thee, my dear one, thee, my daughter — who
    Art ignorant of what thou art: nought knowing
    Of whence I am, nor that I am more better
    Than Prospero, master of a full poor cell,
    And thy no greater father.
25 MIRANDA More to know
    Did never meddle with my thoughts.
    PROSPERO 'Tis time
    I should inform thee further. Lend thy hand
    And pluck my magic garment from me. So: *Lays down*
30   Lie there, my art. Wipe thou thine eyes, have   *his magic cloak*
      comfort.
    The direful spectacle of the wreck, which touched
    The very virtue of compassion in thee,
    I have with such provision in mine art
    So safely ordered that there is no soul —
35   No, not so much perdition as an hair
    Betid to any creature in the vessel
    Which thou heard'st cry, which thou saw'st sink.
      Sit down,   *Miranda sits*
    For thou must now know further.
    MIRANDA You have often
40   Begun to tell me what I am, but stopped
    And left me to a bootless inquisition,
    Concluding 'Stay: not yet.'
    PROSPERO The hour's now come,
    The very minute bids thee ope thine ear:
45   Obey, and be attentive. Canst thou remember
    A time before we came unto this cell?
    I do not think thou canst, for then thou wast not
    Out three years old.
    MIRANDA Certainly, sir, I can.
50 PROSPERO By what? By any other house or person?
    Of any thing the image, tell me, that
    Hath kept with thy remembrance.

---

22 **whence I am** where I am from   **more better** of a higher rank   23 **full poor cell** very humble dwelling, often that of a hermit or monk   24 **no greater father** no more important a father than this **cell** suggests 25 **More to know** desire to know more   26 **meddle with** mingle with/intrude upon   33 **provision** foresight   35 **perdition** loss, damage   36 **Betid** happened   41 **bootless inquisition** useless inquiry 44 **ope** open   48 **Out** fully   52 **Hath ... remembrance** remains in your memory

MIRANDA 'Tis far off,
And rather like a dream than an assurance
55   That my remembrance warrants. Had I not
Four or five women once that tended me?
PROSPERO Thou hadst; and more, Miranda. But how is it
That this lives in thy mind? What see'st thou else
In the dark backward and abysm of time?
60   If thou rememb'rest aught ere thou cam'st here,
How thou cam'st here thou mayst.
MIRANDA But that I do not.
PROSPERO Twelve year since, Miranda, twelve year since,
Thy father was the Duke of Milan and
65   A prince of power.
MIRANDA Sir, are not you my father?
PROSPERO Thy mother was a piece of virtue, and
She said thou wast my daughter; and thy father
Was Duke of Milan, and his only heir
70   And princess, no worse issued.
MIRANDA O the heavens!
What foul play had we, that we came from thence?
Or blessèd wast we did?
PROSPERO Both, both, my girl.
75   By foul play — as thou say'st — were we heaved
      thence,
But blessedly holp hither.
MIRANDA O, my heart bleeds
To think o'th'teen that I have turned you to,
Which is from my remembrance. Please you, further.
80 PROSPERO My brother and thy uncle, called Antonio —
I pray thee, mark me — that a brother should
Be so perfidious — he whom next thyself
Of all the world I loved, and to him put
The manage of my state, as at that time
85   Through all the signories it was the first,
And Prospero the prime duke, being so reputed
In dignity, and for the liberal arts
Without a parallel; those being all my study,   ·
The government I cast upon my brother

---

54 **assurance** certainty   55 **warrants** guarantees   56 **tended** cared for/waited upon   59 **backward** past period **abysm** abyss, gulf   60 **aught** anything   67 **piece** exemplar, image   70 **no worse issued** (you are) of no less noble birth   73 **blessèd** fortunate   76 **holp** helped   78 **o'th'teen** of the trouble **turned you to** caused you   79 **from** absent from   81 **mark** pay attention to   82 **perfidious** treacherous
84 **manage** management   85 **signories** domains/governing bodies of Italian states   86 **prime** foremost
87 **liberal arts** seven scholastic disciplines: grammar, logic, rhetoric, music, astronomy, geometry, arithmetic

90   And to my state grew stranger, being transported
        And rapt in secret studies. Thy false uncle —
        Dost thou attend me?

MIRANDA Sir, most heedfully.

PROSPERO Being once perfected how to grant suits,
95   How to deny them, who t'advance and who
        To trash for over-topping, new created
        The creatures that were mine, I say, or changed 'em,
        Or else new formed 'em; having both the key
        Of officer and office, set all hearts i'th'state
100   To what tune pleased his ear, that now he was
        The ivy which had hid my princely trunk
        And sucked my verdure out on't.— Thou attend'st
           not.

MIRANDA O good sir, I do.

PROSPERO I pray thee, mark me:
105   I, thus neglecting worldly ends, all dedicated
        To closeness and the bettering of my mind
        With that, which but by being so retired,
        O'er-prized all popular rate, in my false brother
        Awaked an evil nature, and my trust,
110   Like a good parent, did beget of him
        A falsehood in its contrary, as great
        As my trust was, which had indeed no limit,
        A confidence *sans* bound. He being thus lorded,
        Not only with what my revenue yielded,
115   But what my power might else exact: like one
        Who having into truth, by telling of it,
        Made such a sinner of his memory
        To credit his own lie, he did believe
        He was indeed the duke, out o'th'substitution
120   And executing th'outward face of royalty

---

90 state country/role as duke   **stranger** estranged   **transported And rapt** absorbed and enraptured
94 perfected skilled (in)   **suits** petitions, requests   **96 trash for over-topping** rein in for being overly
ambitious   **new ... mine** promoted or gave new positions to Prospero's officials (**creatures**)   **97 changed
'em** substituted others for them/altered their duties   **98 new formed 'em** created new positions/changed
their allegiances   **key** control (plays on senses of 'musical key' and 'tuning key')   **100 that** so that
101 ivy ... trunk the rapid growth of ivy on a tree's trunk can choke or poison the tree   **102 verdure** sap/
vitality/power   **105 worldly ends** i.e. state or governmental duties   **106 closeness** solitude   **107 but**
only   **retired** secluded, secret   **108 O'er-prized ... rate** outstripped the people's understanding/was too
precious for the people to value   **110 good parent** 'good parents breed bad children' (proverbial)   **beget of**
breed in   **111 falsehood ... contrary** deception which, in its opposing nature, was   **113 *sans*** without
lorded made lord   **115 else exact** otherwise demand   **one ... lie** i.e. one who has lied so frequently that
he has made his memory false (**a sinner**) by coming to believe in his own lies   **116 into** unto   **it** i.e. the
lie   **119 out o'th'substitution** as a result of having usurped me   **120 th'outward face** the appearance

With all prerogative: hence his ambition growing —
Dost thou hear?

MIRANDA Your tale, sir, would cure deafness.

PROSPERO To have no screen between this part he
          played,

125   And him he played it for, he needs will be
          Absolute Milan. Me — poor man — my library
          Was dukedom large enough: of temporal royalties
          He thinks me now incapable. Confederates —
          So dry he was for sway — wi'th'King of Naples

130   To give him annual tribute, do him homage,
          Subject his coronet to his crown, and bend
          The dukedom yet unbowed — alas, poor Milan —
          To most ignoble stooping.

MIRANDA O the heavens!

135 **PROSPERO** Mark his condition and th'event, then tell me
          If this might be a brother.

MIRANDA   I should sin
          To think but nobly of my grandmother:
          Good wombs have borne bad sons.

140 **PROSPERO** Now the condition.
          This King of Naples, being an enemy
          To me inveterate, hearkens my brother's suit,
          Which was, that he, in lieu o'th'premises
          Of homage, and I know not how much tribute,

145   Should presently extirpate me and mine
          Out of the dukedom, and confer fair Milan,
          With all the honours, on my brother: whereon,
          A treacherous army levied, one midnight
          Fated to th'purpose, did Antonio open

150   The gates of Milan, and i'th'dead of darkness
          The ministers for th'purpose hurried thence
          Me and thy crying self.

MIRANDA Alack, for pity!
          I, not rememb'ring how I cried out then,

---

124 **screen** separation/obstacle   125 **him** i.e. himself; Antonio benefits from playing the role of duke
126 **Absolute Milan** wholly the Duke of Milan and wielding absolute power   127 **temporal royalties**
practical concerns of state   128 **Confederates** (he) conspires   129 **dry** thirsty, desperate   **sway** power
130 **tribute** payment of an agreed sum   131 **Subject ... crown** subject himself to Alonso, the king (a duke
wore a **coronet**)   132 **yet** as yet   135 **condition** pact/disposition   **event** outcome   136 **If ... brother** if
this might be the action of a brother/if I might be the brother to such a man   138 **but** anything but
142 **inveterate** long-standing   **hearkens** listens to   143 **he** i.e. the King of Naples   **in ... homage** in
return for the conditions of allegiance/servility   144 **tribute** money   145 **presently extirpate** immediately
uproot   151 **ministers** agents   **thence** away

155   Will cry it o'er again: it is a hint
          That wrings mine eyes to't.
          PROSPERO Hear a little further,
          And then I'll bring thee to the present business
          Which now's upon's: without the which, this story
160   Were most impertinent.
          MIRANDA Wherefore did they not
          That hour destroy us?
          PROSPERO Well demanded, wench:
          My tale provokes that question. Dear, they durst not,
165   So dear the love my people bore me: nor set
          A mark so bloody on the business: but
          With colours fairer, painted their foul ends.
          In few, they hurried us aboard a barque,
          Bore us some leagues to sea, where they prepared
170   A rotten carcass of a butt, not rigged,
          Nor tackle, sail, nor mast: the very rats
          Instinctively have quit it. There they hoist us,
          To cry to th'sea that roared to us; to sigh
          To th'winds, whose pity sighing back again,
175   Did us but loving wrong.
          MIRANDA Alack, what trouble
          Was I then to you!
          PROSPERO O, a cherubin
          Thou wast that did preserve me. Thou didst smile,
180   Infusèd with a fortitude from heaven,
          When I have decked the sea with drops full salt,
          Under my burden groaned, which raised in me
          An undergoing stomach, to bear up
          Against what should ensue.
185   **MIRANDA** How came we ashore?   *Prospero sits*
          PROSPERO By providence divine.
          Some food we had, and some fresh water, that
          A noble Neapolitan, Gonzalo,
          Out of his charity — who being then appointed
190   Master of this design — did give us, with
          Rich garments, linens, stuffs and necessaries,
          Which since have steaded much. So, of
            his gentleness,

---

155 hint experience/occasion   **160 impertinent** irrelevant   **164 durst** dared   **167 painted** dressed up, disguised   **168 few** brief   **barque** small ship   **170 butt** barrel   **172 hoist** launched   **175 loving wrong** i.e. although they blew us to sea, the winds pitied us   **178 cherubin** angel   **181 decked** covered/adorned   **drops full salt** i.e. tears   **182 which** i.e. Miranda's smile   **183 undergoing stomach** courage to endure   **190 design** plan   **191 stuffs** equipment, provisions   **192 steaded much** been very useful **gentleness** nobleness

Knowing I loved my books, he furnished me
From mine own library with volumes that
195   I prize above my dukedom.

MIRANDA Would I might
But ever see that man.

PROSPERO Now I arise: *Prospero stands*
Sit still, and hear the last of our sea-sorrow.
200   Here in this island we arrived, and here
Have I, thy schoolmaster, made thee more profit
Than other princes can that have more time
For vainer hours, and tutors not so careful.

MIRANDA Heavens thank you for't. And now, I pray
        you, sir,
205   For still 'tis beating in my mind: your reason
For raising this sea-storm?

PROSPERO Know thus far forth:
By accident most strange, bountiful Fortune —
Now my dear lady — hath mine enemies
210   Brought to this shore: and by my prescience
I find my zenith doth depend upon
A most auspicious star, whose influence
If now I court not, but omit, my fortunes
Will ever after droop. Here cease more questions:
215   Thou art inclined to sleep. 'Tis a good dullness,
And give it way: I know thou canst not choose.—   *Miranda sleeps*
Come away, servant, come. I am ready now.
Approach, my Ariel, come.
Enter Ariel

ARIEL All hail, great master! Grave sir, hail! I come
220   To answer thy best pleasure; be't to fly,
To swim, to dive into the fire, to ride
On the curled clouds: to thy strong bidding task
Ariel and all his quality.

PROSPERO Hast thou, spirit,
225   Performed to point the tempest that I bade thee?

---

196 Would I wish   199 Sit still remain seated   201 more profit benefit far more   203 vainer more
idle   careful caring/painstaking   209 my dear lady i.e. Fortune   210 prescience foresight/visionary
power   211 zenith peak of fortune (literally, highest point of the heavens)   212 influence power/invisible
substance supposed to stream from stars and affect one's destiny   213 omit ignore   215 dullness
sleepiness   216 it way in to it   218 Ariel as well as having connotations of 'airiness', the name is Hebrew
for 'lion of God'; also the name of a magical spirit in various occult texts; perhaps evocative of the archangel
Uriel   219 Grave learned, respected, dignified   222 task instruct   223 quality skills/other spirits   225 to
point in every respect

ARIEL To every article.
      I boarded the king's ship: now on the beak,
      Now in the waist, the deck, in every cabin,
      I flamed amazement: sometime I'd divide
230   And burn in many places; on the topmast,
      The yards and bowsprit would I flame distinctly,
      Then meet and join. Jove's lightning, the precursors
      O'th'dreadful thunderclaps, more momentary
      And sight-outrunning were not; the fire and cracks
235   Of sulphurous roaring, the most mighty Neptune
      Seem to besiege and make his bold waves tremble,
      Yea, his dread trident shake.
PROSPERO My brave spirit!
      Who was so firm, so constant, that this coil
240   Would not infect his reason?
ARIEL Not a soul
      But felt a fever of the mad and played
      Some tricks of desperation. All but mariners
      Plunged in the foaming brine and quit the vessel,
245   Then all afire with me: the king's son, Ferdinand,
      With hair up-staring — then like reeds, not hair —
      Was the first man that leaped; cried 'Hell is empty
      And all the devils are here.'
PROSPERO Why, that's my spirit!
250   But was not this nigh shore?
ARIEL Close by, my master.
PROSPERO But are they, Ariel, safe?
ARIEL Not a hair perished:
      On their sustaining garments not a blemish,
255   But fresher than before: and, as thou bad'st me,
      In troops I have dispersed them 'bout the isle.
      The king's son have I landed by himself,
      Whom I left cooling of the air with sighs
      In an odd angle of the isle, and sitting,
260   His arms in this sad knot.   *Folds his arms*

---

227 beak prow **228 waist** middle **229 flamed amazement** appeared as a terrifying fire **231 yards** crossbars on masts **bowsprit** long pole that holds a sail **232 Jove's ... thunderclaps** thunder and lightning were the chief weapons of the king of the gods **234 sight-outrunning** quicker than the eye can follow **235 Neptune** Roman god of the sea **237 trident** three-pronged spear, carried by **Neptune**
239 coil turmoil **242 of the mad** such as mad people suffer **played ... desperation** displayed symptoms of despair, recklessness **245 all afire** i.e. the ship caught fire **246 up-staring** standing on end **250 nigh** near **254 sustaining** necessary/buoyant **256 troops** groups **258 cooling of** cooling **259 angle** nook, corner **260 sad knot** i.e. folded, a sign of melancholy

PROSPERO Of the king's ship,
    The mariners, say how thou hast disposed,
    And all the rest o'th'fleet?
ARIEL Safely in harbour
265   Is the king's ship: in the deep nook where once
    Thou call'dst me up at midnight to fetch dew
    From the still-vexed Bermudas, there she's hid;
    The mariners all under hatches stowed,
    Who, with a charm joined to their suffered labour,
270   I have left asleep: and for the rest o'th'fleet —
    Which I dispersed — they all have met again,
    And are upon the Mediterranean float
    Bound sadly home for Naples,
    Supposing that they saw the king's ship wrecked
275   And his great person perish.
PROSPERO Ariel, thy charge
    Exactly is performed; but there's more work:
    What is the time o'th'day?
ARIEL Past the mid season.
280 PROSPERO At least two glasses. The time 'twixt six
      and now
    Must by us both be spent most preciously.
ARIEL Is there more toil? Since thou dost give me pains,
    Let me remember thee what thou hast promised,
    Which is not yet performed me.
285 PROSPERO How now? Moody?
    What is't thou canst demand?
ARIEL My liberty.
PROSPERO Before the time be out? No more!
ARIEL I prithee,
290   Remember I have done thee worthy service,
    Told thee no lies, made thee no mistakings, served
    Without or grudge or grumblings: thou did promise
    To bate me a full year.
PROSPERO Dost thou forget
295   From what a torment I did free thee?
ARIEL No.

---

266 **dew** a common ingredient of magic potions   267 **still-vexed Bermudas** the Bermuda islands were famed for fearful storms   268 **under hatches** i.e. below deck   269 **charm** spell   **suffered labour** i.e. the tiring work performed during the storm   272 **float** sea   279 **mid season** noon   280 **two glasses** two hourglasses (so it is about 2 p.m.)   281 **preciously** valuably   282 **pains** work, effort   283 **remember** remind 285 **Moody?** ill-humoured/stubborn/wilful   288 **time be out** fixed period of service is over   292 **or** either 293 **bate me** deduct from my term of service

PROSPERO Thou dost: and think'st it much to tread
    the ooze
    Of the salt deep,
    To run upon the sharp wind of the north,
300   To do me business in the veins o'th'earth
    When it is baked with frost.

ARIEL I do not, sir.

PROSPERO Thou liest, malignant thing. Hast thou forgot
    The foul witch Sycorax, who with age and envy
305   Was grown into a hoop? Hast thou forgot her?

ARIEL No, sir.

PROSPERO Thou hast. Where was she born? Speak:
    tell me.

ARIEL Sir, in Algiers.

PROSPERO O, was she so? I must
310   Once in a month recount what thou hast been,
    Which thou forget'st. This damned witch Sycorax,
    For mischiefs manifold, and sorceries terrible
    To enter human hearing, from Algiers,
    Thou know'st, was banished: for one thing she did
315   They would not take her life. Is not this true?

ARIEL Ay, sir.

PROSPERO This blue-eyed hag was hither brought
    with child,
    And here was left by th'sailors. Thou, my slave,
    As thou report'st thyself, was then her servant:
320   And, for thou wast a spirit too delicate
    To act her earthy and abhorred commands,
    Refusing her grand hests, she did confine thee
    By help of her more potent ministers,
    And in her most unmitigable rage,
325   Into a cloven pine, within which rift
    Imprisoned thou didst painfully remain
    A dozen years: within which space she died,
    And left thee there, where thou didst vent thy groans
    As fast as mill-wheels strike. Then was this island —

---

297 **tread … deep** walk on the muddy sand of the ocean floor   304 **Sycorax** name of uncertain origin,
possibly derived from Greek *sus* ('pig') and *korax* ('raven'), animals associated with witchcraft   305 **hoop** i.e.
bent posture   308 **Algiers** seaport capital of Algeria, in North Africa   314 **for … life** probably meaning
that Sycorax was pregnant and therefore could not be executed   317 **blue-eyed** with dark circles under the
eyes or with blue eyelids, thought to be a sign of pregnancy   **hag** witch   **with child** pregnant   320 **for**
because   **delicate** fine in quality/ethereal   321 **earthy** coarse/of the earth   322 **hests** commands
323 **ministers** assistants   324 **unmitigable** impossible to assuage   325 **cloven** cleft, split   329 **As …**
strike as often as each blade of a water-wheel hits the water

330 Save for the son that she did litter here,
A freckled whelp, hag-born — not honoured with
A human shape.
ARIEL Yes: Caliban her son.
PROSPERO Dull thing, I say so: he, that Caliban
335 Whom now I keep in service. Thou best know'st
What torment I did find thee in: thy groans
Did make wolves howl and penetrate the breasts
Of ever-angry bears; it was a torment
To lay upon the damned, which Sycorax
340 Could not again undo. It was mine art,
When I arrived and heard thee, that made gape
The pine and let thee out.
ARIEL I thank thee, master.
PROSPERO If thou more murmur'st, I will rend an oak
345 And peg thee in his knotty entrails till
Thou hast howled away twelve winters.
ARIEL Pardon, master:
I will be correspondent to command
And do my spriting gently.
350 **PROSPERO** Do so: and after two days
I will discharge thee.
ARIEL That's my noble master!
What shall I do? Say what? What shall I do?
PROSPERO Go make thyself like a nymph o'th'sea,
355 Be subject to no sight but thine and mine: invisible
To every eyeball else. Go take this shape
And hither come in't: go! Hence with diligence!

Exit [*Ariel*]

Awake, dear heart, awake. Thou hast slept well.
Awake.   *To Miranda*
MIRANDA The strangeness of your story put
360 Heaviness in me.
PROSPERO Shake it off. Come on:
We'll visit Caliban, my slave, who never
Yields us kind answer.
MIRANDA 'Tis a villain, sir, I do not love to look on.

---

330 **litter** give birth to (term applied to animals)   331 **whelp** puppy, son of a bitch   **hag-born** born of a witch   333 **Caliban** anagram of 'can[n]ibal'; perhaps derived from the Romany word *caulibon* ('dark thing')   334 **Dull thing** may refer to Ariel or Caliban   335 **in service** as a servant   337 **wolves . . . bears** i.e. even moved fierce beasts   341 **gape** open   344 **murmur'st** complain   **rend** tear apart   345 **peg** fasten   **entrails** innards (literally, intestines)   348 **correspondent** responsive, obedient   349 **spriting** magical actions of a sprite (spirit)   **gently** quietly, tamely   351 **discharge** free   360 **Heaviness** sleepiness   364 **villain** base, low-born/wicked person

365 PROSPERO But, as 'tis,
        We cannot miss him: he does make our fire,
        Fetch in our wood and serves in offices
        That profit us. What, ho! Slave! Caliban!
        Thou earth, thou! Speak!
370 CALIBAN There's wood enough within.   *Within*
     PROSPERO Come forth, I say! There's other business
        for thee:
        Come, thou tortoise! When?
     Enter Ariel like a water-nymph
        Fine apparition: my quaint Ariel,
        Hark in thine ear.
375 ARIEL My lord, it shall be done.   *Exit*
     PROSPERO Thou poisonous slave, got by the devil
        himself
        Upon thy wicked dam: come forth!
     Enter Caliban
     CALIBAN As wicked dew as e'er my mother brushed
        With raven's feather from unwholesome fen
380   Drop on you both! A southwest blow on ye
        And blister you all o'er!
     PROSPERO For this, be sure, tonight thou shalt have
        cramps,
        Side-stitches that shall pen thy breath up: urchins
        Shall, for that vast of night that they may work,
385   All exercise on thee: thou shalt be pinched
        As thick as honeycomb, each pinch more stinging
        Than bees that made 'em.
     CALIBAN I must eat my dinner.
        This island's mine by Sycorax my mother,
390   Which thou tak'st from me. When thou cam'st first,
        Thou strok'st me and made much of me: wouldst
        give me
        Water with berries in't, and teach me how
        To name the bigger light, and how the less,
        That burn by day and night: and then I loved thee
395   And showed thee all the qualities o'th'isle,

---

366 miss do without   **367 offices** duties   **369 earth** earthy thing/low creature/piece of dirt   **373 quaint** ingenious/elegant   **376 got** conceived   **377 dam** mother   **379 fen** swampy ground   **380 southwest** winds from the south-west were thought to bring damp, disease-ridden air   **383 urchins** hedgehogs/spirits in hedgehog form   **384 vast** expanse/long period   **385 exercise** work   **386 As ... honeycomb** i.e. as many times as there are cells in a honeycomb/so that you resemble a honeycomb   **387 Than** than the **'em** i.e. honeycombs   **392 berries** possibly grapes to make a mild wine, or juniper berries, which would create a kind of gin   **393 bigger ... less** i.e. the sun and moon

The fresh springs, brine-pits, barren place and fertile.
Cursed be I that did so! All the charms
Of Sycorax — toads, beetles, bats — light on you!
For I am all the subjects that you have,
400   Which first was mine own king: and here you sty me
In this hard rock, whiles you do keep from me
The rest o'th'island.

PROSPERO Thou most lying slave,
    Whom stripes may move, not kindness! I have
      used thee —
405   Filth as thou art — with humane care, and
      lodged thee
In mine own cell, till thou didst seek to violate
The honour of my child.

CALIBAN O ho, O ho! Would't had been done!
    Thou didst prevent me: I had peopled else
410   This isle with Calibans.

MIRANDA Abhorrèd slave,
    Which any print of goodness wilt not take,
    Being capable of all ill. I pitied thee,
    Took pains to make thee speak, taught thee each
      hour
415   One thing or other: when thou didst not, savage,
Know thine own meaning, but wouldst gabble like
A thing most brutish, I endowed thy purposes
With words that made them known. But thy vile
    race —
Though thou didst learn — had that in't which
    good natures
420   Could not abide to be with: therefore wast thou
Deservedly confined into this rock, who hadst
Deserved more than a prison.

CALIBAN You taught me language, and my profit on't
    Is, I know how to curse. The red-plague rid you
425   For learning me your language.

PROSPERO Hag-seed, hence!
    Fetch us in fuel, and be quick: thou'rt best
To answer other business. Shrug'st thou, malice?

---

396 **brine-pits** pools of salt water   397 **charms** spells   398 **light** alight   400 **sty** pen up, confine
401 **hard rock** cave   404 **stripes** lashes of a whip   **kindness** good will/natural feeling/kinship   404 **used**
treated   405 **humane** human/benevolent   406 **violate . . . child** i.e. rape Miranda   409 **I . . . else** otherwise
I would have populated   412 **print** imprint, image   413 **capable . . . ill** only susceptible to evil/able to perform
any kind of evil   418 **race** innate disposition   422 **more** more punishment   424 **red-plague** red sores were
caused by, amongst other diseases, the plague   **rid** destroy   425 **learning** teaching   426 **Hag-seed** offspring
of a witch   427 **thou'rt best** you would be better off

If thou neglect'st or dost unwillingly
430 What I command, I'll rack thee with old cramps,
Fill all thy bones with aches, make thee roar,
That beasts shall tremble at thy din.

CALIBAN No, pray thee.—
I must obey: his art is of such power,   *Aside*
435 It would control my dam's god, Setebos,
And make a vassal of him.

PROSPERO So, slave, hence!   *Exit Caliban*
Enter Ferdinand, and Ariel, invisible, playing and singing

ARIEL Come unto these yellow sands,   *Song*
And then take hands:
440 Curtsied when you have, and kissed
The wild waves whist:
Foot it featly here and there,
And, sweet sprites, bear
The burden.

[**SPIRITS** *Within, sing the*] (*burden, dispersedly*)
445 Hark, hark! Bow-wow!
The watch-dogs bark: bow-wow.

ARIEL Hark, hark! I hear
The strain of strutting chanticleer
Cry, cock-a-diddle-dow.

450 **FERDINAND** Where should this music be? I'th'air or
th'earth?
It sounds no more: and sure it waits upon
Some god o'th'island. Sitting on a bank,
Weeping again the king my father's wreck,
This music crept by me upon the waters,
455 Allaying both their fury and my passion
With its sweet air: thence I have followed it —
Or it hath drawn me rather — but 'tis gone.
No, it begins again.

ARIEL Full fathom five thy father lies,   *Song*
460 Of his bones are coral made:
Those are pearls that were his eyes:
Nothing of him that doth fade,
But doth suffer a sea-change

---

430 rack torture   **old cramps** plentiful cramps/cramps of old age/cramps similar to those Caliban has experienced previously   **435 Setebos** a Patagonian god mentioned in sixteenth-century travel narratives   **436 vassal** servant, slave   **441 whist** (become) silent   **442 Foot it featly** dance skilfully   **444 *burden*** chorus, refrain   **448 strain** song   **chanticleer** rooster   **451 waits upon** attends/anticipates   **453 the** for the   **455 passion** acute grief   **459 fathom five** five fathoms (thirty feet) deep   **462 fade** decompose   **463 suffer** undergo

Into something rich and strange.
465   Sea-nymphs hourly ring his knell:
[**SPIRITS** *Within, sing the*] (*burden*) Ding-dong.
ARIEL Hark! Now I hear them: ding-dong, bell.
FERDINAND The ditty does remember my drowned
      father.
      This is no mortal business, nor no sound
470   That the earth owes. I hear it now above me.
PROSPERO The fringèd curtains of thine eye advance
      And say what thou see'st yond.
MIRANDA What is't? A spirit?
      Lord, how it looks about! Believe me, sir,
475   It carries a brave form. But 'tis a spirit.
PROSPERO No, wench: it eats, and sleeps, and hath
      such senses
      As we have, such. This gallant which thou see'st
      Was in the wreck: and, but he's something stained
      With grief — that's beauty's canker — thou
      mightst call him
480   A goodly person: he hath lost his fellows
      And strays about to find 'em.
MIRANDA I might call him
      A thing divine, for nothing natural
      I ever saw so noble.
485 **PROSPERO** It goes on, I see,   *Aside*
      As my soul prompts it.— Spirit, fine spirit: I'll free
      thee   *To Ariel*
      Within two days for this.
FERDINAND Most sure, the goddess
      On whom these airs attend! Vouchsafe my prayer
490   May know if you remain upon this island,
      And that you will some good instruction give
      How I may bear me here: my prime request,
      Which I do last pronounce, is — O you wonder! —
      If you be maid or no?
495 **MIRANDA** No wonder, sir,
      But certainly a maid.

---

465 knell funeral bell **468 ditty** song/lyrics **does remember** recalls/commemorates **469 mortal** human (plays on the sense of 'deathly') **470 owes** owns **471 fringèd curtains** i.e. eyelids **advance** open **472 yond** yonder, over there **475 brave** handsome, noble, splendid **477 gallant** fashionable, handsome young man **478 but** except that **something** somewhat **479 canker** infection, corruption **480 goodly** handsome, fine **483 natural** human **486 prompts** directs, urges, wills **489 airs** Ariel's songs **Vouchsafe** grant (that) **490 remain** live **492 bear me** behave **493 wonder** plays on the Latin root of Miranda's name ('*mirandus*' – i.e. 'wonderful') **494 maid** human/a virgin, unmarried

FERDINAND My language? Heavens!
I am the best of them that speak this speech,
Were I but where 'tis spoken.

500 PROSPERO How? The best?
What wert thou if the King of Naples heard thee?

FERDINAND A single thing, as I am now, that wonders
To hear thee speak of Naples. He does hear me:
And that he does, I weep. Myself am Naples,
505 Who with mine eyes, never since at ebb, beheld
The king my father wrecked.

MIRANDA Alack, for mercy!

FERDINAND Yes, faith, and all his lords, the Duke of
Milan
And his brave son being twain.

510 PROSPERO The Duke of Milan   *Aside*
And his more braver daughter could control thee
If now 'twere fit to do't. At the first sight
They have changed eyes.— Delicate Ariel,   *To Ariel*
I'll set thee free for this.— A word, good sir,   *To Ferdinand*
515 I fear you have done yourself some wrong: a word.

MIRANDA Why speaks my father so ungently? This
Is the third man that e'er I saw: the first
That e'er I sighed for. Pity move my father
To be inclined my way.

520 FERDINAND O, if a virgin,
And your affection not gone forth, I'll make you
The Queen of Naples.

PROSPERO Soft, sir, one word more.—
They are both in either's powers: but this swift
business   *Aside*
525 I must uneasy make, lest too light winning
Make the prize light.— One word more: I charge thee   *To Ferdinand*
That thou attend me: thou dost here usurp
The name thou ow'st not, and hast put thyself

---

498 **best** i.e. highest in rank (a king, assuming his father is drowned)   499 **where 'tis spoken** i.e. Naples
502 **A single thing** solitary/a bachelor/one and the same person (as the King of Naples)   503 **He** i.e. as I am
now king and hear my own grief   505 **ebb** low tide (i.e. without tears)   509 **son** Antonio's son is never
mentioned again: perhaps Shakespeare forgot or cut the part, neglecting this reference   **twain** separated
511 **control** challenge/govern   513 **changed eyes** gazed at one another, exchanged loving looks
Delicate fine/ethereal   515 **done … wrong** i.e. spoken falsely in your claim to be king   516 **ungently**
harshly/discourteously   521 **your … forth** you have not fallen in love with or betrothed yourself to
someone else   523 **Soft** wait a moment   524 **either's** each other's   525 **uneasy** difficult   **light** easy, but
in the next line the sense shifts to 'less valuable/unchaste'   526 **charge** command   527 **attend** listen to,
take heed of   528 **ow'st not** do not own

Upon this island as a spy, to win it
530 From me, the lord on't.
FERDINAND No, as I am a man.
MIRANDA There's nothing ill can dwell in such a temple:
If the ill-spirit have so fair a house,
Good things will strive to dwell with't.
535 PROSPERO Follow me.—   *To Ferdinand*
Speak not you for him: he's a traitor.— Come: *To Miranda/To*
I'll manacle thy neck and feet together: *Ferdinand*
Seawater shalt thou drink: thy food shall be
The fresh-brook mussels, withered roots and husks
540 Wherein the acorn cradled. Follow.
FERDINAND No!
I will resist such entertainment till
Mine enemy has more power.
He draws, and is charmed from moving
MIRANDA O dear father,
545 Make not too rash a trial of him, for
He's gentle, and not fearful.
PROSPERO What, I say,
My foot my tutor?— Put thy sword up, traitor: *To Ferdinand*
Who mak'st a show but dar'st not strike, thy
conscience
550 Is so possessed with guilt. Come from thy ward,
For I can here disarm thee with this stick,   *Brandishes his staff*
And make thy weapon drop.
MIRANDA Beseech you, father.   *Kneels or attempts*
PROSPERO Hence! Hang not on my garments.   *to stop him*
555 MIRANDA Sir, have pity:
I'll be his surety.
PROSPERO Silence! One word more
Shall make me chide thee, if not hate thee. What,
An advocate for an impostor? Hush!
560 Thou think'st there is no more such shapes as he,
Having seen but him and Caliban. Foolish wench,
To th'most of men this is a Caliban,
And they to him are angels.

---

530 **on't** of it (the island)   532 **temple** i.e. Ferdinand's body   539 **fresh-brook mussels** inedible
freshwater mussels   542 **entertainment** treatment/hospitality   546 **gentle** noble/courteous   **fearful**
frightening   548 **foot** i.e. inferior body part (proverbial: 'do not make the foot the head')   550 **ward**
defensive posture   556 **surety** guarantor   558 **chide** scold/punish   560 **shapes** i.e. men   562 **To**
compared to

MIRANDA My affections
565   Are then most humble: I have no ambition
    To see a goodlier man.
PROSPERO Come on, obey: *To Ferdinand*
    Thy nerves are in their infancy again
    And have no vigour in them.
570 FERDINAND So they are:
    My spirits, as in a dream, are all bound up.
    My father's loss, the weakness which I feel,
    The wreck of all my friends, nor this man's threats,
    To whom I am subdued, are but light to me,
575   Might I but through my prison once a day
    Behold this maid: all corners else o'th'earth
    Let liberty make use of: space enough
    Have I in such a prison.
PROSPERO It works.— Come on.—   *Aside/To Ferd.*
580   Thou hast done well, fine Ariel!— Follow me.—   *To Ariel/To Ferd.*
    Hark what thou else shalt do me.   *To Ariel*
MIRANDA Be of comfort:
    My father's of a better nature, sir,
    Than he appears by speech: this is unwonted
585   Which now came from him.
PROSPERO Thou shalt be as free   *To Ariel*
    As mountain winds; but then exactly do
    All points of my command.
ARIEL To th'syllable.
590 PROSPERO Come, follow.— Speak not for him.   *To Ferd./To Mir.*
                                Exeunt

Act 2 Scene 1   *running scene 3*

Enter Alonso, Sebastian, Antonio, Gonzalo, Adrian,
Francisco and others

GONZALO Beseech you, sir, be merry; you have cause —   *To Alonso*
    So have we all — of joy, for our escape
    Is much beyond our loss. Our hint of woe
    Is common: every day some sailor's wife,
5   The masters of some merchant, and the merchant
    Have just our theme of woe. But for the miracle —

---

568 **nerves** sinews, muscles   569 **vigour** strength   571 **spirits** vital powers/senses   575 **through** i.e.
from   576 **all corners else** everywhere else   581 **do me** do for me   584 **unwonted** uncharacteristic
587 **then** i.e. if that is to be the case   2.1   3 **Is much beyond** far outweighs **hint** circumstance, occasion
5 **masters … merchant** officers of some merchant ship

I mean our preservation — few in millions
Can speak like us: then wisely, good sir, weigh
Our sorrow with our comfort.

10 ALONSO Prithee, peace.

SEBASTIAN He receives comfort like cold porridge.   *Antonio and*

ANTONIO The visitor will not give him o'er so.   *Sebastian speak*

SEBASTIAN Look, he's winding up the watch of his wit: *apart*
by and by it will strike.

15 GONZALO Sir—   *To Alonso*

SEBASTIAN One: tell.

GONZALO When every grief is entertained that's offered,
comes to th'entertainer—

SEBASTIAN A dollar.   *Aside to Antonio,*

20 GONZALO Dolour comes to him, indeed: you have   *but overheard by*
spoken truer than you purposed.   *Gonzalo*

SEBASTIAN You have taken it wiselier than I meant you
should.

GONZALO Therefore, my lord—   *To Alonso*

25 ANTONIO Fie, what a spendthrift is he of his tongue!

ALONSO I prithee, spare.   *To Gonzalo*

GONZALO Well, I have done: but yet—

SEBASTIAN He will be talking.

ANTONIO Which, of he or Adrian, for a good wager, first

30 begins to crow?

SEBASTIAN The old cock.

ANTONIO The cockerel.

SEBASTIAN Done. The wager?

ANTONIO A laughter.

35 SEBASTIAN A match!

ADRIAN Though this island seem to be desert—

SEBASTIAN Ha, ha, ha!

ANTONIO So: you're paid.

ADRIAN Uninhabitable and almost inaccessible—

40 SEBASTIAN Yet—

ADRIAN Yet—

---

8 **weigh** balance   10 **peace** possibly Sebastian puns on 'peas' by introducing **porridge**, a vegetable
stew   12 **visitor** charitable visitor offering comfort or advice   13 **wit** intelligence   16 **tell** count (the strokes)
17 **entertained** received   19 **dollar** large silver coin (playing on the sense of **entertainer** as 'performer')
20 **Dolour** sorrow   21 **purposed** intended   22 **wiselier** more profoundly/wittily   26 **spare** desist
30 **crow** i.e. speak   32 **cockerel** young cock/young man   33 **wager** bet, stake   34 **A laughter** 'he wins
that laughs' (proverbial); may also play on the sense of 'the whole number of eggs laid by a hen before she is
ready to sit'   36 **desert** deserted   37 **Ha … paid** most editors assume that the speakers of these two lines
should be reversed, so that Antonio wins the bet and laughs, then Sebastian replies that the laugh pays off
the debt; but it could be that Sebastian laughs in response to Adrian's words (*seems deserted? – of course* it's
deserted) and that by doing so he has paid off the bet

ANTONIO He could not miss't.

ADRIAN It must needs be of subtle, tender and delicate temperance.

45 **ANTONIO** Temperance was a delicate wench.

SEBASTIAN Ay, and a subtle, as he most learnedly delivered.

ADRIAN The air breathes upon us here most sweetly.

SEBASTIAN As if it had lungs, and rotten ones.

50 **ANTONIO** Or as 'twere perfumed by a fen.

GONZALO Here is everything advantageous to life.

ANTONIO True: save means to live.

SEBASTIAN Of that there's none, or little.

GONZALO How lush and lusty the grass looks. How
55 green!

ANTONIO The ground indeed is tawny.

SEBASTIAN With an eye of green in't.

ANTONIO He misses not much.

SEBASTIAN No: he doth but mistake the truth totally.

60 **GONZALO** But the rarity of it is — which is indeed almost beyond credit—

SEBASTIAN As many vouched rarities are.

GONZALO —That our garments, being, as they were, drenched in the sea, hold notwithstanding their
65 freshness and glosses, being rather new-dyed than stained with salt water.

ANTONIO If but one of his pockets could speak, would it not say he lies?

SEBASTIAN Ay, or very falsely pocket up his report.

70 **GONZALO** Methinks our garments are now as fresh as when we put them on first in Afric, at the marriage of the king's fair daughter Claribel to the King of Tunis.

SEBASTIAN 'Twas a sweet marriage, and we prosper well in our return.

75 **ADRIAN** Tunis was never graced before with such a paragon to their queen.

GONZALO Not since widow Dido's time.

---

43 **subtle** refined   44 **temperance** moderate climate (Antonio's response treats **Temperance** as the name of a woman)   45 **delicate** pleasure-seeking, voluptuous   46 **subtle** crafty/sexually experienced   **learnedly delivered** uttered authoritatively   50 **fen** bog, marshland   52 **save** except   54 **lusty** of vigorous growth   56 **tawny** yellowish brown   57 **eye** tinge   60 **rarity** exceptional nature   61 **credit** belief   62 **vouched** acknowledged   65 **new-dyed** brand new   69 **pocket up** conceal   71 **Afric** Africa   72 **Tunis** North African city, now the capital of Tunisia   77 **Dido's** Dido, Queen of Carthage, was the widow of Sychaeus, but was famed for her love affair with **Aeneas**; she committed suicide when he left her; there may also be a lewd pun on the slang term 'dido' (genitals/dildo)

ANTONIO Widow! A pox o'that! How came that 'widow'
   in? Widow Dido!

80 SEBASTIAN What if he had said 'widower Aeneas' too?
   Good lord, how you take it!

ADRIAN 'Widow Dido', said you? You make me study of
   that: she was of Carthage, not of Tunis.

GONZALO This Tunis, sir, was Carthage.

85 ADRIAN Carthage?

GONZALO I assure you, Carthage.

ANTONIO His word is more than the miraculous harp.

SEBASTIAN He hath raised the wall and houses too.

ANTONIO What impossible matter will he make easy
90 next?

SEBASTIAN I think he will carry this island home in his
   pocket and give it his son for an apple.

ANTONIO And, sowing the kernels of it in the sea, bring
   forth more islands.

95 GONZALO Ay.

ANTONIO Why, in good time.

GONZALO Sir, we were talking that our garments seem   *To Alonso*
   now as fresh as when we were at Tunis at the
   marriage of your daughter, who is now queen.

100 ANTONIO And the rarest that e'er came there.

SEBASTIAN Bate, I beseech you, widow Dido.

ANTONIO O, widow Dido? Ay, widow Dido.

GONZALO Is not, sir, my doublet as fresh as the first day
   I wore it? I mean, in a sort—

105 ANTONIO That sort was well fished for.

GONZALO —When I wore it at your daughter's
   marriage.

ALONSO You cram these words into mine ears against
   The stomach of my sense. Would I had never
110 Married my daughter there: for, coming thence,
   My son is lost and — in my rate — she too,
   Who is so far from Italy removed
   I ne'er again shall see her. O thou mine heir

79 How ... in? Antonio contests the reference to an abandoned woman as a widow   80 'widower Aeneas'
Aeneas had been married to Creusa, who died in the sack of Troy   82 study of examine, meditate on
84 This ... Carthage Tunis was about ten miles from Carthage and became the most important city in the
region after Carthage fell   87 miraculous harp in Greek mythology, Amphion's music caused the walls of
Thebes to rebuild themselves   93 kernels pips   100 rarest most splendid/beautiful   101 Bate disregard
102 Ay, widow Dido if there is a missing speech prefix, this could be a cynical interjection from Sebastian
103 doublet close-fitting jacket   104 in a sort to some extent   105 sort perhaps a reference to the
drawing of lots or to the 'sorting' of fish for market   109 stomach appetite/inclination   sense disposition
111 rate opinion

Of Naples and of Milan, what strange fish
115   Hath made his meal on thee?

FRANCISCO Sir, he may live:
I saw him beat the surges under him,
And ride upon their backs; he trod the water,
Whose enmity he flung aside, and breasted
120   The surge most swoll'n that met him: his bold head
'Bove the contentious waves he kept, and oared
Himself with his good arms in lusty stroke
To th'shore, that o'er his wave-worn basis bowed,
As stooping to relieve him: I not doubt
125   He came alive to land.

ALONSO No, no, he's gone.

SEBASTIAN Sir, you may thank yourself for this great   *To Alonso*
loss,
That would not bless our Europe with your daughter,
But rather loose her to an African,
130   Where she, at least, is banished from your eye,
Who hath cause to wet the grief on't.

ALONSO Prithee, peace.

SEBASTIAN You were kneeled to and importuned
otherwise
By all of us: and the fair soul herself
135   Weighed between loathness and obedience at
Which end o'th'beam should bow. We have lost
your son,
I fear, forever: Milan and Naples have
More widows in them of this business' making
Than we bring men to comfort them.
140   The fault's your own.

ALONSO So is the dear'st o'th'loss.

GONZALO My lord Sebastian,
The truth you speak doth lack some gentleness,
And time to speak it in: you rub the sore,
145   When you should bring the plaster.

SEBASTIAN Very well.

ANTONIO And most chirurgeonly.

---

117 **surges** waves   121 **oared** rowed   122 **lusty** vigorous   123 **wave-worn basis** the eroded base of the
cliff rising from the **shore**   124 **As** as if   129 **loose** release, turn loose (as one would an animal)
131 **Who** probably applies to Alonso's eye, but possibly to Claribel   **wet the grief** weep   133 **importuned**
pleaded with   135 **loathness** loathing, repulsion   136 **which ... bow** which half of the scales should
sink   141 **dear'st** most precious/significant part (i.e. Ferdinand)   144 **time** i.e. appropriate time
147 **chirurgeonly** surgeon-like

GONZALO It is foul weather in us all, good sir,   *To Alonso*
    When you are cloudy.
150 SEBASTIAN Foul weather?
    ANTONIO Very foul.
    GONZALO Had I plantation of this isle, my lord—
    ANTONIO He'd sow't with nettle-seed.
    SEBASTIAN Or docks, or mallows.
155 GONZALO And were the king on't, what would I do?
    SEBASTIAN Scape being drunk for want of wine.
    GONZALO I'th'commonwealth I would by contraries
        Execute all things: for no kind of traffic
        Would I admit: no name of magistrate:
160   Letters should not be known: riches, poverty,
        And use of service, none: contract, succession,
        Bourn, bound of land, tilth, vineyard, none:
        No use of metal, corn, or wine, or oil:
        No occupation, all men idle, all:
165   And women too, but innocent and pure:
        No sovereignty.
    SEBASTIAN Yet he would be king on't.
    ANTONIO The latter end of his commonwealth forgets
        the beginning.
    GONZALO All things in common nature should produce
170   Without sweat or endeavour: treason, felony,
        Sword, pike, knife, gun, or need of any engine,
        Would I not have: but nature should bring forth,
        Of it own kind, all foison, all abundance,
        To feed my innocent people.
175 SEBASTIAN No marrying 'mong his subjects?
    ANTONIO None, man, all idle: whores and knaves.
    GONZALO I would with such perfection govern, sir,
        T'excel the golden age.
    SEBASTIAN 'Save his majesty!
180 ANTONIO Long live Gonzalo!   *Bowing or*
    GONZALO And — do you mark me, sir?   *doffing hats*
    ALONSO Prithee, no more: thou dost talk nothing to me.
    GONZALO I do well believe your highness: and did it to
        minister occasion to these gentlemen, who are of

152 **plantation** opportunity for colonization (Antonio plays on the sense of 'planting')   153 **nettle-seed** . . .
mallows common wild plants/weeds   156 **want** lack   157 **by . . . things** implement the opposite to what is
usual   158 **traffic** trade, commerce   160 **Letters** scholarship, learning   161 **use of service** practice of
having servants   **succession** inheritance   162 **Bourn** land boundary   **tilth** farmed land   169 **in
common** communal   171 **pike** spear   **engine** device/machinery/weapon   173 **foison** plenty
178 **golden age** in classical mythology, the earliest of ages, when life was idyllic   181 **mark** hear, observe
184 **minister occasion** provide an opportunity (for laughter)

185 such sensible and nimble lungs that they always use
to laugh at nothing.

ANTONIO 'Twas you we laughed at.

GONZALO Who in this kind of merry fooling am nothing
to you: so you may continue and laugh at nothing
190 still.

ANTONIO What a blow was there given!

SEBASTIAN An it had not fallen flat-long.

GONZALO You are gentlemen of brave metal: you would
lift the moon out of her sphere, if she would continue
195 in it five weeks without changing.

Enter Ariel [invisible] playing solemn music

SEBASTIAN We would so, and then go a-batfowling.

ANTONIO Nay, good my lord, be not angry.

GONZALO No, I warrant you: I will not adventure my
discretion so weakly. Will you laugh me asleep, for
200 I am very heavy?

ANTONIO Go sleep, and hear us.   *All sleep except*

ALONSO What, all so soon asleep? I wish mine eyes   *Alonso, Sebastian*
Would, with themselves, shut up my thoughts.   *and Antonio*
I find they are inclined to do so.

205 **SEBASTIAN** Please you, sir,
Do not omit the heavy offer of it.
It seldom visits sorrow: when it doth, it is a
comforter.

ANTONIO We two, my lord, will guard your person
While you take your rest, and watch your safety.

210 **ALONSO** Thank you. Wondrous heavy.   *He sleeps*

SEBASTIAN What a strange drowsiness possesses them!
[*Exit Ariel*]

ANTONIO It is the quality o'th'climate.

SEBASTIAN Why
Doth it not then our eyelids sink? I find
215 Not myself disposed to sleep.

ANTONIO Nor I: my spirits are nimble.
They fell together all, as by consent
They dropped, as by a thunder-stroke. What might,

---

185 sensible responsive, sensitive   **nimble** agile, swift to respond   **use** are accustomed   **192 An … flat-long** if it had not been delivered with the flat side of the sword (rather than the sharp edge)   **193 metal** puns on 'mettle' (constitution, courage)   **194 sphere** position in the heavens   **195 five weeks** i.e. rather than the usual four, which ought to be long enough   **196 a-batfowling** catching roosting birds/swindling   **198 warrant** assure   **adventure … weakly** risk my sound judgement for such a slight cause   **200 heavy** drowsy   **206 omit** reject, ignore   **it** i.e. sleep   **217 as** as if

Worthy Sebastian? O, what might? — No more.—
220 And yet, methinks I see it in thy face,
What thou shouldst be: th'occasion speaks thee, and
My strong imagination sees a crown
Dropping upon thy head.

SEBASTIAN What? Art thou waking?

225 **ANTONIO** Do you not hear me speak?

SEBASTIAN I do, and surely
It is a sleepy language and thou speak'st
Out of thy sleep. What is it thou didst say?
This is a strange repose, to be asleep
230 With eyes wide open: standing, speaking, moving,
And yet so fast asleep.

ANTONIO Noble Sebastian,
Thou let'st thy fortune sleep — die, rather: wink'st
Whiles thou art waking.

235 **SEBASTIAN** Thou dost snore distinctly:
There's meaning in thy snores.

ANTONIO I am more serious than my custom: you
Must be so too, if heed me: which to do
Trebles thee o'er.

240 **SEBASTIAN** Well, I am standing water.

ANTONIO I'll teach you how to flow.

SEBASTIAN Do so: to ebb
Hereditary sloth instructs me.

ANTONIO O,
245 If you but knew how you the purpose cherish
Whiles thus you mock it: how in stripping it
You more invest it. Ebbing men, indeed,
Most often, do so near the bottom run
By their own fear, or sloth.

250 **SEBASTIAN** Prithee, say on:
The setting of thine eye and cheek proclaim
A matter from thee; and a birth, indeed,
Which throes thee much to yield.

ANTONIO Thus, sir:
255 Although this lord of weak remembrance, this,

---

221 th'occasion speaks the opportunity speaks to   **224 waking** awake   **233 wink'st** shut your eyes (i.e.
refuse to see what is in front of you)   **235 distinctly** meaningfully, clearly   **237 custom** usual self
238 heed you heed   **239 Trebles thee o'er** makes you three times greater   **240 standing water** not
ebbing or flowing (i.e. open to ideas/idle)   **243 Hereditary sloth** natural laziness/my position as younger
brother to a king   **245 If … it** if only you realized that your mockery reveals your intentions/if only you
realized that despite your mockery you harbour genuine desires   **247 invest** clothe, adorn   **Ebbing**
declining   **250 say on** speak more, go on   **251 setting** look/fixed appearance   **252 matter** issue of
importance   **253 throes … yield** gives you much pain to bring forth   **255 lord** i.e. Gonzalo
remembrance memory

Who shall be of as little memory
When he is earthed, hath here almost persuaded —
For he's a spirit of persuasion, only
Professes to persuade — the king his son's alive:
260 'Tis as impossible that he's undrowned
As he that sleeps here swims.

SEBASTIAN I have no hope
That he's undrowned.

ANTONIO O, out of that 'no hope'
265 What great hope have you! No hope that way is
Another way so high a hope, that even
Ambition cannot pierce a wink beyond,
But doubt discovery there. Will you grant with me
That Ferdinand is drowned?

270 **SEBASTIAN** He's gone.

ANTONIO Then, tell me: who's the next heir of Naples?

SEBASTIAN Claribel.

ANTONIO She that is Queen of Tunis: she that dwells
Ten leagues beyond man's life: she that from Naples
275 Can have no note, unless the sun were post —
The man i'th'moon's too slow — till new-born chins
Be rough and razorable: she that from whom
We all were sea-swallowed, though some cast again —
And by that destiny — to perform an act
280 Whereof what's past is prologue, what to come
In yours and my discharge.

SEBASTIAN What stuff is this? How say you?
'Tis true, my brother's daughter's Queen of Tunis:
So is she heir of Naples, 'twixt which regions
285 There is some space.

ANTONIO A space whose every cubit
Seems to cry out, 'How shall that Claribel
Measure us back to Naples? Keep in Tunis,
And let Sebastian wake.' Say this were death
290 That now hath seized them: why, they were
no worse

256 **of … memory** as little remembered   257 **earthed** dead and buried   258 **a spirit of** expert at, the epitome of   **only Professes** (as an adviser) makes it his sole vocation   266 **high a hope** i.e. of gaining the crown   267 **Ambition … there** ambition itself could not glimpse it and doubt that there is anything to achieve/ambition itself could not ordinarily proceed a fraction further without fear of discovery
274 **leagues** a league was about three miles   **man's life** a lifetime's journey   275 **note** communication/information   **post** messenger   277 **from whom** i.e. returning from whose wedding   278 **cast** vomited up   280 **Whereof … prologue** in relation to which all that has gone before is only a prelude to what is to come   281 **discharge** performance/management   282 **stuff** notion/rubbish   285 **space** distance
286 **cubit** about twenty inches (the length of the forearm)   288 **Measure us back** travel back over us (i.e. retrace her steps)   **Keep** remain   289 **wake** i.e. to his opportunity

Than now they are. There be that can rule Naples
As well as he that sleeps: lords that can prate
As amply and unnecessarily
As this Gonzalo: I myself could make
295 A chough of as deep chat. O, that you bore
The mind that I do! What a sleep were this
For your advancement! Do you understand me?

SEBASTIAN Methinks I do.

ANTONIO And how does your content
300 Tender your own good fortune?

SEBASTIAN I remember
You did supplant your brother Prospero.

ANTONIO True:
And look how well my garments sit upon me,
305 Much feater than before. My brother's servants
Were then my fellows: now they are my men.

SEBASTIAN But for your conscience.

ANTONIO Ay, sir: where lies that? If 'twere a kibe,
'Twould put me to my slipper: but I feel not
310 This deity in my bosom: twenty consciences
That stand 'twixt me and Milan, candied be they,
And melt ere they molest! Here lies your brother,
No better than the earth he lies upon,
If he were that which now he's like — that's dead —
315 Whom I with this obedient steel — three inches   *Touching*
    of it —   *sword or dagger*
Can lay to bed forever: whiles you, doing thus,
To the perpetual wink for aye might put
This ancient morsel, this Sir Prudence, who
Should not upbraid our course. For all the rest,
320 They'll take suggestion as a cat laps milk:
They'll tell the clock to any business that
We say befits the hour.

SEBASTIAN Thy case, dear friend,
Shall be my precedent. As thou got'st Milan,
325 I'll come by Naples. Draw thy sword: one stroke

---

292 he i.e. Alonso   **prate** prattle   **294 make … chat** train a jackdaw to be as profound   **295 bore … do**
shared my intention/were of my way of thinking/were resolved like me   **299 content** liking   **300 Tender**
value, regard   **302 supplant** overthrow   **304 garments** i.e. his duke's robes   **305 feater** with a better
fit   **306 fellows** companions, equals   **men** servants   **308 kibe** chilblain, blister   **309 put me to** force me
to wear   **310 deity** i.e. conscience   **311 candied** made of ice, crystallized   **317 perpetual wink** endless
sleep   **aye** ever   **318 morsel** piece of flesh/scrap   **319 Should not** must not be allowed to   **321 tell …
hour** declare it is whatever time we require/agree to any business that we propose

Shall free thee from the tribute which thou payest,
And I the king shall love thee.

ANTONIO Draw together:
And when I rear my hand, do you the like,
330 To fall it on Gonzalo.

SEBASTIAN O, but one word.   *They talk apart*

Enter Ariel [invisible] with music and song

ARIEL My master through his art foresees the danger   *To Gonzalo,*
That you, his friend, are in, and sends me forth —   *who still sleeps*
For else his project dies — to keep them living.
335 While you here do snoring lie, *Sings in Gonzalo's ear*
Open-eyed conspiracy
His time doth take.
If of life you keep a care,
Shake off slumber, and beware:
340 Awake, awake!

ANTONIO Then let us both be sudden.   *Antonio and Sebastian*
draw their swords

GONZALO Now, good angels preserve the king!   *Waking*

ALONSO Why, how now? Ho, awake! Why are you   *The others wake*
drawn?
Wherefore this ghastly looking?

345 **GONZALO** What's the matter?

SEBASTIAN Whiles we stood here securing your repose,
Even now, we heard a hollow burst of bellowing
Like bulls, or rather lions: did't not wake you?
It struck mine ear most terribly.

350 **ALONSO** I heard nothing.

ANTONIO O, 'twas a din to fright a monster's ear,
To make an earthquake! Sure it was the roar
Of a whole herd of lions.

ALONSO Heard you this, Gonzalo?

355 **GONZALO** Upon mine honour, sir, I heard a humming,
And that a strange one too, which did awake me:
I shaked you, sir, and cried: as mine eyes opened,
I saw their weapons drawn: there was a noise,
That's verily. 'Tis best we stand upon our guard,
360 Or that we quit this place: let's draw our weapons.

ALONSO Lead off this ground, and let's make further
search
For my poor son.

---

326 tribute annual sum payable by Antonio to Naples in return for receiving Alonso's help in deposing
Prospero **329 rear** raise **334 project** plan **337 time** opportunity **344 ghastly** full of fear **359 verily**
certain

GONZALO Heavens keep him from these beasts!
    For he is sure i'th'island.
365 ALONSO Lead away.
ARIEL Prospero, my lord, shall know what I have done.
    So, king, go safely on to seek thy son.

Exeunt [separately]

Act 2 Scene 2 *running scene 4*

*Enter Caliban with a burden of wood. A noise of thunder
heard*

CALIBAN All the infections that the sun sucks up
    From bogs, fens, flats, on Prosper fall, and make him
    By inch-meal a disease. His spirits hear me,
    And yet I needs must curse. But they'll nor pinch,
5   Fright me with urchin-shows, pitch me i'th'mire,
    Nor lead me like a firebrand in the dark
    Out of my way, unless he bid 'em: but
    For every trifle are they set upon me,
    Sometime like apes, that mow and chatter at me,
10 And after bite me: then like hedgehogs, which
    Lie tumbling in my barefoot way and mount
    Their pricks at my footfall: sometime am I
    All wound with adders, who with cloven tongues
    Do hiss me into madness.
Enter Trinculo

                  Lo, now, lo!
15 Here comes a spirit of his, and to torment me
    For bringing wood in slowly. I'll fall flat:
    Perchance he will not mind me.   *Lies down and*
TRINCULO Here's neither bush nor shrub to bear off any   *covers himself*
    weather at all, and another storm brewing: I hear it   *with his cloak*
20 sing i'th'wind: yond same black cloud, yond huge
    one, looks like a foul bombard that would shed his
    liquor. If it should thunder as it did before, I know not
    where to hide my head: yond same cloud cannot
    choose but fall by pailfuls. What have we here? A   *Sees Caliban*
25 man or a fish? Dead or alive? A fish, he smells like a
    fish: a very ancient and fishlike smell: a kind of

2.2 **2 flats** plain, swampy ground **3 By inch-meal** inch by inch **4 nor** neither **pinch** torment
5 urchin-shows goblin apparitions **6 firebrand** will-o'-the-wisp, moving light **9 mow** grimace, make
faces **13 wound** wound round **cloven** split/forked *Trinculo* perhaps from the Italian *trincare* ('to drink
eagerly') **14 Lo** look **17 mind** notice **18 bear off** ward off **21 bombard** leather wine jug

not-of-the-newest poor-John. A strange fish! Were I in
England now — as once I was — and had but this
fish painted, not a holiday fool there but would give a
30   piece of silver: there would this monster make a man:
any strange beast there makes a man: when they will
not give a doit to relieve a lame beggar, they will lay
out ten to see a dead Indian. Legged like a man and
his fins like arms! Warm, o'my troth! I do now let
35   loose my opinion, hold it no longer: this is no fish, but
an islander that hath lately suffered by a thunderbolt.   *Thunder*
Alas, the storm is come again! My best way is to
creep under his gaberdine: there is no other
shelter hereabout. Misery acquaints a man with
40   strange bedfellows: I will here shroud till the dregs of   *Trinculo gets*
the storm be past.   *under Caliban's cloak*
Enter Stephano, singing   *With a bottle*
STEPHANO I shall no more to sea, to sea: *in his hand*
     Here shall I die ashore—
This is a very scurvy tune to sing at a man's funeral:
45   well, here's my comfort.   *Drinks*
     The master, the swabber, the boatswain and I,   *Sings*
     The gunner and his mate,
     Loved Mall, Meg and Marian and Margery,
     But none of us cared for Kate.
50   For she had a tongue with a tang,
     Would cry to a sailor, 'Go hang!'
     She loved not the savour of tar nor of pitch,
     Yet a tailor might scratch her where'er she did itch:
     Then to sea, boys, and let her go hang!
55   This is a scurvy tune too: but here's my comfort.
                                                     Drinks

CALIBAN Do not torment me: O!

STEPHANO What's the matter? Have we devils here? Do
you put tricks upon's with savages and men of Ind,
ha? I have not scaped drowning to be afeard now
60   of your four legs: for it hath been said, 'As proper a
man as ever went on four legs, cannot make him give

---

27 poor-John dried hake, a fish mainly eaten by the poor   **29 fish painted** i.e. on a sign to attract passers-by
30 make a man make a man rich/be taken for a man   **32 doit** trifling sum (a small Dutch coin)   **33 dead
Indian** American Indians were sometimes displayed to the paying public   **Legged** with legs   **34 let loose**
take back   **38 gaberdine** coarse-textured cloak   **40 shroud** shelter   **44 scurvy** wretched, disagreeable
46 swabber sailor who washes the deck   **50 tang** sting   **52 savour** smell   **53 tailor . . . itch** she would let
a tailor (proverbially lecherous) have sex with her (**itch** may suggest venereal disease)   **57 the matter**
happening   **58 Ind** India   **60 proper** normal/fine   **61 four legs** Stephano sees the legs of both Trinculo
and Caliban and adapts a common proverb   **give ground** yield

ground': and it shall be said so again, while Stephano breathes at'nostrils.

CALIBAN The spirit torments me: O!

65 **STEPHANO** This is some monster of the isle with four legs, who hath got, as I take it, an ague. Where the devil should he learn our language? I will give him some relief, if it be but for that. If I can recover him, and keep him tame, and get to Naples with him, he's a
70 present for any emperor that ever trod on neat's leather.

CALIBAN Do not torment me, prithee: I'll bring my wood home faster.

STEPHANO He's in his fit now, and does not talk after the
75 wisest. He shall taste of my bottle: if he have never drunk wine afore, it will go near to remove his fit. If I can recover him and keep him tame, I will not take too much for him: he shall pay for him that hath him, and that soundly.

80 **CALIBAN** Thou dost me yet but little hurt: thou wilt anon, I know it by thy trembling. Now Prosper works upon thee.

STEPHANO Come on your ways: open your mouth: here is that which will give language to you, cat. Open
85 your mouth: this will shake your shaking, I can tell   *Gives Caliban*
you, and that soundly: you cannot tell who's your   *a drink*
friend: open your chaps again.   *Caliban spits it out*

TRINCULO I should know that voice: it should be— but he is drowned, and these are devils. O, defend me!

90 **STEPHANO** Four legs and two voices: a most delicate monster! His forward voice now is to speak well of his friend: his backward voice is to utter foul speeches and to detract. If all the wine in my bottle will recover him, I will help his ague. Come. Amen! I will
95 pour some in thy other mouth.

TRINCULO Stephano!

STEPHANO Doth thy other mouth call me? Mercy, mercy! This is a devil, and no monster: I will leave him, I have no long spoon.

---

63 **at'nostrils** through his nostrils   66 **ague** sickness, shaking, fever   68 **relief** refreshment, sustenance **recover** revive   70 **neat's leather** cowhide   74 **after** in the manner of   77 **I ... him** i.e. no price can be too high for him   81 **anon** shortly   83 **Come ... ways** come on/come here   84 **language ... cat** 'ale will make a cat speak' (proverbial)   85 **shake** cast off   87 **chaps** jaws   90 **delicate** extraordinary/ingeniously made/delightful   93 **detract** slander   99 **long spoon** 'he should have a long spoon that sups with the devil' (proverbial)

100 **TRINCULO** Stephano! If thou be'st Stephano, touch me and speak to me, for I am Trinculo — be not afeard — thy good friend Trinculo.

STEPHANO If thou be'st Trinculo, come forth: I'll pull thee by the lesser legs. If any be Trinculo's legs, these *Pulls him out*

105 are they. Thou art very Trinculo indeed! How cam'st thou to be the siege of this moon-calf? Can he vent Trinculos?

TRINCULO I took him to be killed with a thunder-stroke: but art thou not drowned, Stephano? I hope now

110 thou art not drowned: is the storm overblown? I hid me under the dead moon-calf's gaberdine for fear of the storm: and art thou living, Stephano? O Stephano, two Neapolitans scaped! *Trinculo and Stephano embrace*

STEPHANO Prithee, do not turn me about: my stomach is *or dance*

115 not constant.

CALIBAN These be fine things, an if they be not sprites. *Aside* That's a brave god and bears celestial liquor: I will kneel to him.

STEPHANO How didst thou scape? How cam'st thou

120 hither? Swear by this bottle how thou cam'st hither. I escaped upon a butt of sack which the sailors heaved o'erboard, by this bottle which I made of the bark of a tree with mine own hands since I was cast ashore.

125 **CALIBAN** I'll swear upon that bottle to be thy true subject, for the liquor is not earthly.

STEPHANO Here: swear then how thou escap'dst.

TRINCULO Swum ashore, man, like a duck: I can swim like a duck, I'll be sworn.

130 **STEPHANO** Here, kiss the book. Though thou canst swim *Gives Trinculo* like a duck, thou art made like a goose. *the bottle*

TRINCULO O Stephano, hast any more of this?

STEPHANO The whole butt, man: my cellar is in a rock by th'sea-side, where my wine is hid.— How now, *To Caliban*

135 moon-calf? How does thine ague?

CALIBAN Hast thou not dropped from heaven?

---

104 lesser legs presumably Trinculo has shorter legs than Caliban   **106 siege** excrement (Stephano pulls Trinculo out from between Caliban's legs)   **moon-calf** monstrosity, misshapen creature, idiot (born under the moon's influence)   **vent** discharge/fart   **110 overblown** blown over   **116 an if** if   **121 butt of sack** barrel of Spanish white wine   **130 kiss the book** alludes to kissing the Bible to confirm an oath, and to the phrase 'kiss the cup' (i.e. 'have another drink')   **131 goose** simpleton; also suggests drunken giddiness

STEPHANO Out o'th'moon, I do assure thee: I was the
man i'th'moon when time was.

CALIBAN I have seen thee in her, and I do adore thee: my
140   mistress showed me thee, and thy dog, and thy bush.

STEPHANO Come, swear to that: kiss the book: I will   *Gives Caliban*
furnish it anon with new contents. Swear.   *the bottle*
                                                              Caliban drinks
                                                                    Aside?

TRINCULO By this good light, this is a very shallow
monster! I afeard of him? A very weak monster! The
145   man i'th'moon? A most poor, credulous monster!
Well drawn, monster, in good sooth!

CALIBAN I'll show thee every fertile inch o'th'island: and
I will kiss thy foot. I prithee, be my god.

TRINCULO By this light, a most perfidious and drunken   *Aside?*
150   monster! When's god's asleep, he'll rob his bottle.

CALIBAN I'll kiss thy foot: I'll swear myself thy subject.

STEPHANO Come on then: down, and swear.   *Caliban kneels*

TRINCULO I shall laugh myself to death at this puppy-   *Aside?*
headed monster. A most scurvy monster! I could find
155   in my heart to beat him—

STEPHANO Come, kiss.   *To Caliban*

TRINCULO —But that the poor monster's in drink: an
abominable monster!

CALIBAN I'll show thee the best springs: I'll pluck thee
160   berries: I'll fish for thee and get thee wood enough. A
plague upon the tyrant that I serve! I'll bear him no
more sticks, but follow thee, thou wondrous man.

TRINCULO A most ridiculous monster, to make a wonder   *Aside?*
of a poor drunkard!

165 CALIBAN I prithee, let me bring thee where crabs grow:
and I with my long nails will dig thee pignuts: show
thee a jay's nest and instruct thee how to snare the
nimble marmoset: I'll bring thee to clust'ring filberts,
and sometimes I'll get thee young scamels from the
170   rock. Wilt thou go with me?

STEPHANO I prithee, now lead the way without any
more talking. Trinculo, the king and all our company

---

138 when time was once   139 adore worship   140 mistress i.e. Miranda   dog . . . bush in folklore, the
man in the moon had been banished there with his dog after he illegally gathered kindling (his **bush**) on a
Sunday   142 new contents i.e. more wine   143 good light i.e. the sun   shallow gullible, naïve
146 drawn drunk   sooth truth   149 perfidious treacherous   153 puppy-headed stupid   157 in drink
drunk   165 crabs crab-apples   166 pignuts edible roots, earth chestnuts   168 marmoset small monkey
filberts hazelnuts   169 scamels of uncertain meaning; perhaps error for 'seamews' (seagulls) or 'shamois'
(goat); a fish or shellfish has also been suggested, but **rock** and **young** go better with the goatish sense

else being drowned, we will inherit here.— Here,   *To Caliban*
bear my bottle. Fellow Trinculo, we'll fill him by
175   and by again.

CALIBAN Farewell master: farewell, farewell!

Sings drunkenly

TRINCULO A howling monster: a drunken monster!

CALIBAN No more dams I'll make for fish,   *Sings*
Nor fetch in firing at requiring,
180   Nor scrape trencher, nor wash dish,
'Ban, 'Ban, Cacaliban
Has a new master: get a new man.
Freedom, high-day! High-day, freedom! Freedom,
high-day, freedom!

185   STEPHANO O brave monster, lead the way!

Exeunt

Act 3 Scene 1   *running scene 5*

Enter Ferdinand, bearing a log

FERDINAND There be some sports are painful, and
their labour   *Sets down*
Delight in them sets off: some kinds of baseness   *the log*
Are nobly undergone, and most poor matters
Point to rich ends. This my mean task
5   Would be as heavy to me as odious, but
The mistress which I serve quickens what's dead
And makes my labours pleasures: O, she is
Ten times more gentle than her father's crabbed;
And he's composed of harshness. I must remove
10   Some thousands of these logs and pile them up,
Upon a sore injunction. My sweet mistress
Weeps when she sees me work and says such
baseness
Had never like executor. I forget:
But these sweet thoughts do even refresh my labours, *Picks up the log*
15   Most busy least, when I do it.

Enter Miranda and Prospero   *Prospero at a*
distance, unseen

178 **for** i.e. to trap   179 **firing** firewood   180 **trencher** wooden plate   183 **high-day** holiday
3.1   1 sports activities, pastimes   **painful** arduous   **their … off** the pleasure derived from the task is
enhanced by the hard work/pleasure in undertaking the task removes the sense of effort   **2 baseness**
contemptible work   **4 mean** lowly   **6 quickens** enlivens   **8 crabbed** irritable, churlish   **11 sore
injunction** severe command   **12 such … executor** such a lowly task has never had such a performer
13 forget forget to work   **15 Most busy least** being busy seems like being at leisure, thanks to **sweet
thoughts** of Miranda

MIRANDA Alas, now pray you,   *To Ferdinand*
      Work not so hard. I would the lightning had
      Burnt up those logs that you are enjoined to pile.
      Pray, set it down and rest you: when this burns
20   'Twill weep for having wearied you. My father
      Is hard at study: pray now, rest yourself,
      He's safe for these three hours.
FERDINAND O most dear mistress,
      The sun will set before I shall discharge
25   What I must strive to do.
MIRANDA If you'll sit down,
      I'll bear your logs the while: pray give me that,
      I'll carry it to the pile.
FERDINAND No, precious creature,
30   I had rather crack my sinews, break my back,
      Than you should such dishonour undergo,
      While I sit lazy by.
MIRANDA It would become me
      As well as it does you; and I should do it
35   With much more ease, for my good will is to it,
      And yours it is against.
PROSPERO Poor worm, thou art infected.   *Aside*
      This visitation shows it.
MIRANDA You look wearily.
40   FERDINAND No, noble mistress, 'tis fresh morning
            with me
      When you are by at night. I do beseech you,
      Chiefly that I might set it in my prayers,
      What is your name?
MIRANDA Miranda.— O my father,
45   I have broke your hest to say so.
FERDINAND Admired Miranda,
      Indeed the top of admiration, worth
      What's dearest to the world! Full many a lady
      I have eyed with best regard, and many a time
50   Th'harmony of their tongues hath into bondage
      Brought my too diligent ear. For several virtues
      Have I liked several women, never any
      With so full soul but some defect in her
      Did quarrel with the noblest grace she owed,

---

18 enjoined bound   **20 weep** by releasing drops of moisture or resin   **24 discharge** carry out
33 become be fitting for   **37 infected** with love   **38 visitation** visit (plays on senses of 'bout of plague' and
'charitable visit to the poor')   **41 by** nearby   **45 hest** command   **47 top** epitome, pinnacle   **50 bondage**
slavery   **51 diligent** attentive   **54 owed** owned

55   And put it to the foil. But you, O you,
        So perfect and so peerless, are created
        Of every creature's best.

MIRANDA I do not know
        One of my sex; no woman's face remember,
60   Save from my glass, mine own: nor have I seen
        More that I may call men than you, good friend,
        And my dear father: how features are abroad,
        I am skilless of; but by my modesty —
        The jewel in my dower — I would not wish
65   Any companion in the world but you:
        Nor can imagination form a shape
        Besides yourself to like of. But I prattle
        Something too wildly, and my father's precepts
        I therein do forget.

70   **FERDINAND** I am in my condition
        A prince, Miranda: I do think, a king —
        I would not so — and would no more endure
        This wooden slavery than to suffer
        The flesh-fly blow my mouth. Hear my soul speak:
75   The very instant that I saw you, did
        My heart fly to your service, there resides
        To make me slave to it, and for your sake
        Am I this patient log-man.

MIRANDA Do you love me?

80   **FERDINAND** O heaven, O earth, bear witness to this
                sound,
        And crown what I profess with kind event
        If I speak true: if hollowly, invert
        What best is boded me to mischief: I,
        Beyond all limit of what else i'th'world,
85   Do love, prize, honour you.

MIRANDA I am a fool
        To weep at what I am glad of.

PROSPERO Fair encounter   *Aside*
        Of two most rare affections! Heavens rain grace
90   On that which breeds between 'em.

FERDINAND Wherefore weep you?

---

55 **put … foil** thwarted it/disputed it (as in a swordfight)   60 **glass** mirror   61 **friend** lover
62 **how … abroad** what people look like in the world   63 **skilless** ignorant   **modesty** virtue, chastity
64 **dower** dowry   68 **precepts** instructions, orders   70 **condition** social rank   74 **flesh-fly** fly that lays
its eggs in dead flesh   **blow** contaminate/deposit eggs in/swell   81 **kind event** favourable outcome
82 **hollowly** insincerely   83 **boded** intended   **mischief** misfortune, harm   84 **what** whatever   88 **Fair**
excellent, pleasing   89 **rare** special, profound   90 **that … 'em** that which develops between them/their
children

MIRANDA At mine unworthiness, that dare not offer
    What I desire to give; and much less take
    What I shall die to want. But this is trifling,
95   And all the more it seeks to hide itself
    The bigger bulk it shows. Hence, bashful cunning,
    And prompt me, plain and holy innocence.
    I am your wife, if you will marry me:
    If not, I'll die your maid: to be your fellow
100   You may deny me, but I'll be your servant
    Whether you will or no.
FERDINAND My mistress, dearest,   *Kneels*
    And I thus humble ever.
MIRANDA My husband, then?
105 FERDINAND Ay, with a heart as willing
    As bondage e'er of freedom: here's my hand.
MIRANDA And mine, with my heart in't: and now
          farewell
    Till half an hour hence.
FERDINAND A thousand thousand!
        Exeunt [Ferdinand and Miranda, separately]
110 PROSPERO So glad of this as they I cannot be,
    Who are surprised withal: but my rejoicing
    At nothing can be more. I'll to my book,
    For yet ere supper-time must I perform
    Much business appertaining.   *Exit*

Act 3 Scene 2   *running scene 6*

Enter Caliban, Stephano and Trinculo

STEPHANO Tell not me: when the butt is out we will
    drink water: not a drop before; therefore bear up, and
    board 'em. Servant-monster, drink to me.
TRINCULO Servant-monster? The folly of this island!—   *Aside*
5   They say there's but five upon this isle: we are
    three of them: if th'other two be brained like us, the
    state totters.

---

94 **to want** for lack of   96 **Hence, bashful cunning** away with timid devices/coy artfulness   99 **maid** virgin/servant   **fellow** spouse   102 **mistress** sweetheart   106 **As ... freedom** as slavery embraces freedom   109 **thousand** i.e. farewells   111 **surprised** delightfully bewildered/taken unawares   **withal** by it   **my ... more** nothing could make me rejoice more   114 **appertaining** relevant to this   **3.2   1 Tell not me** presumably to stop drinking   **out** finished   2 **bear up** stay standing/approach   3 **board 'em** get on board/attack (i.e. 'drink up')   6 **brained** furnished with a brain/drunk

STEPHANO Drink, servant-monster, when I bid thee: thy
eyes are almost set in thy head.   *Caliban drinks*

10 TRINCULO Where should they be set else? He were a
brave monster indeed, if they were set in his tail.

STEPHANO My man-monster hath drowned his tongue
in sack: for my part, the sea cannot drown me:
I swam, ere I could recover the shore, five and thirty

15 leagues off and on. By this light, thou shalt be my
lieutenant, monster, or my standard.

TRINCULO Your lieutenant, if you list: he's no standard.

STEPHANO We'll not run, Monsieur Monster.

TRINCULO Nor go neither: but you'll lie like dogs and yet

20 say nothing neither.

STEPHANO Moon-calf, speak once in thy life, if thou be'st
a good moon-calf.

CALIBAN How does thy honour? Let me lick thy shoe. I'll
not serve him: he is not valiant.

25 TRINCULO Thou liest, most ignorant monster: I am in
case to justle a constable. Why, thou deboshed fish
thou, was there ever man a coward that hath drunk
so much sack as I today? Wilt thou tell a monstrous
lie, being but half a fish and half a monster?

30 CALIBAN Lo, how he mocks me! Wilt thou let him, my
lord?

TRINCULO 'Lord', quoth he! That a monster should be
such a natural!

CALIBAN Lo, lo, again! Bite him to death, I prithee.

35 STEPHANO Trinculo, keep a good tongue in your head: if
you prove a mutineer, the next tree. The poor
monster's my subject and he shall not suffer
indignity.

CALIBAN I thank my noble lord. Wilt thou be pleased to

40 hearken once again to the suit I made to thee?

STEPHANO Marry, will I: kneel and repeat it: I will stand,
and so shall Trinculo.

Enter Ariel, invisible

---

9 set drunkenly fixed/glazed (Trinculo plays on the sense of 'placed')   **11 tail** plays on the senses of 'penis' or
'bottom'   **14 recover** reach   **five ... leagues** about 100 miles   **15 off and on** more or less
16 standard ensign or flag-bearer (puns on the sense of 'person capable of standing')   **17 list** wish   **18 run**
i.e. away from battle   **19 go** walk   **lie** lie down/deceive   **24 valiant** worthy/courageous   **26 case** a fit
state, state of readiness   **justle** jostle   **deboshed** debauched, corrupted   **28 monstrous** huge/unnatural/
befitting a monster   **33 natural** simpleton, idiot (plays on the sense of 'normal, naturally formed creature')
35 if ... tree i.e. you'll be hanged like a **mutineer**   **41 Marry** by the Virgin Mary (a mild oath)   **stand** stand
still/listen/remain upright

CALIBAN As I told thee before, I am subject to a tyrant, a
　　sorcerer, that by his cunning hath cheated me of the
45　island.

ARIEL Thou liest.

CALIBAN Thou liest, thou jesting monkey, thou: I would　　*To Trinculo*
　　my valiant master would destroy thee. I do not lie.

STEPHANO Trinculo, if you trouble him any more in's
50　tale, by this hand, I will supplant some of your teeth.

TRINCULO Why, I said nothing.

STEPHANO Mum then, and no more.—　　　　　　　*To Trinculo*
　　Proceed.　　　　　　　　　　　　　　　　　　*To Caliban*

CALIBAN I say by sorcery he got this isle:
55　From me he got it. If thy greatness will
　　Revenge it on him — for I know thou dar'st,
　　But this thing dare not —

STEPHANO That's most certain.

CALIBAN Thou shalt be lord of it, and I'll serve thee.
60　**STEPHANO** How now shall this be compassed?
　　Canst thou bring me to the party?

CALIBAN Yea, yea, my lord: I'll yield him thee asleep,
　　Where thou mayst knock a nail into his head.

ARIEL Thou liest, thou canst not.
65　**CALIBAN** What a pied ninny's this? Thou scurvy patch—　*To Trinculo*
　　I do beseech thy greatness give him blows,　　　　　*To Stephano*
　　And take his bottle from him: when that's gone
　　He shall drink nought but brine, for I'll not show him
　　Where the quick freshes are.
70　**STEPHANO** Trinculo, run into no further danger:
　　interrupt the monster one word further, and by this
　　hand, I'll turn my mercy out o'doors and make a
　　stockfish of thee.

TRINCULO Why, what did I? I did nothing. I'll go further
75　off.

STEPHANO Didst thou not say he lied?

ARIEL Thou liest.

STEPHANO Do I so? Take thou that. As you like this, give　*Beats Trinculo*
　　me the lie another time.

---

44 cunning art, skill, craft　**50 tale** may pun on 'tail,' especially if Trinculo has just kicked Caliban in the
backside　**supplant** uproot (plays on the sense of 'usurp')　**52 Mum** be quiet　**57 this thing** i.e. Trinculo
60 compassed accomplished　**61 party** person in question　**62 yield him thee** deliver him to you
65 pied multicoloured (refers to a jester's clothing)　**patch** fool/clown/rogue　**69 freshes** freshwater
streams　**72 turn … o'doors** banish any feelings of mercy　**73 stockfish** dried cod; Stephano threatens to
beat Trinculo as fish is beaten before cooking; he may also imply that he will take Trinculo's drink away
78 give … lie accuse me of lying/insult me

80 **TRINCULO** I did not give the lie. Out o'your wits and
hearing too? A pox o'your bottle! This can sack and
drinking do: a murrain on your monster, and the
devil take your fingers!

CALIBAN Ha, ha, ha!

85 **STEPHANO** Now, forward with your tale.—   *To Caliban*
Prithee, stand further off.   *To Trinculo*

CALIBAN Beat him enough: after a little time,
I'll beat him too.

STEPHANO Stand further.—   *To Trinculo*

90 Come, proceed.   *To Caliban*

CALIBAN Why, as I told thee, 'tis a custom with him
I'th'afternoon to sleep: there thou mayst brain him,
Having first seized his books: or with a log
Batter his skull, or paunch him with a stake,

95 Or cut his weasand with thy knife. Remember
First to possess his books; for without them
He's but a sot, as I am, nor hath not
One spirit to command: they all do hate him
As rootedly as I. Burn but his books.

100 He has brave utensils — for so he calls them —
Which when he has a house, he'll deck withal.
And that most deeply to consider is
The beauty of his daughter: he himself
Calls her a nonpareil: I never saw a woman,

105 But only Sycorax my dam, and she:
But she as far surpasseth Sycorax
As great'st does least.

STEPHANO Is it so brave a lass?

CALIBAN Ay, lord: she will become thy bed, I warrant,

110 And bring thee forth brave brood.

STEPHANO Monster, I will kill this man: his daughter and
I will be king and queen —'save our graces! — and
Trinculo and thyself shall be viceroys. Dost thou like
the plot, Trinculo?

115 **TRINCULO** Excellent.

STEPHANO Give me thy hand, I am sorry I beat thee: but,
while thou livest, keep a good tongue in thy head.

---

82 murrain plague (literally, disease affecting cattle and sheep)   **85 forward** go on   **87 enough** thoroughly
92 brain him murder him, dash out his brains   **94 paunch** stab in the stomach   **95 weasand** windpipe
97 sot idiot/drunkard   **99 rootedly** deep-seatedly   **100 utensils** instruments of magic or alchemy/
household goods   **101 deck withal** decorate/furnish with   **104 a nonpareil** unsurpassed, one without
equal   **109 become** befit/grace   **110 brood** offspring   **112 'save our graces** God save us
113 viceroys deputy rulers

CALIBAN Within this half hour will he be asleep:
Wilt thou destroy him then?

120 **STEPHANO** Ay, on mine honour.

ARIEL This will I tell my master.   *Aside*

CALIBAN Thou mak'st me merry: I am full of pleasure,
Let us be jocund. Will you troll the catch
You taught me but while-ere?

125 **STEPHANO** At thy request, monster, I will do reason, any
reason: come on, Trinculo, let us sing.

    Flout 'em and scout 'em   *Sings*
    And scout 'em and flout 'em,
    Thought is free.

130 **CALIBAN** That's not the tune.

Ariel plays the tune on a tabor and pipe

STEPHANO What is this same?

TRINCULO This is the tune of our catch, played by the
picture of Nobody.

STEPHANO If thou be'st a man, show thyself in thy

135 likeness: if thou be'st a devil, take't as thou list.

TRINCULO O, forgive me my sins!

STEPHANO He that dies pays all debts: I defy thee. Mercy
upon us!

CALIBAN Art thou afeard?

140 **STEPHANO** No, monster, not I.

CALIBAN Be not afeard, the isle is full of noises,
Sounds and sweet airs, that give delight and hurt not:
Sometimes a thousand twangling instruments
Will hum about mine ears; and sometime voices,

145 That if I then had waked after long sleep,
Will make me sleep again, and then in dreaming,
The clouds methought would open and show riches
Ready to drop upon me, that when I waked
I cried to dream again.

150 **STEPHANO** This will prove a brave kingdom to me, where
I shall have my music for nothing.

CALIBAN When Prospero is destroyed.

STEPHANO That shall be by and by: I remember the
story.   [*Exit Ariel, playing music*]

155 **TRINCULO** The sound is going away: let's follow it, and
after do our work.

---

123 **jocund** joyful **troll** sing merrily **catch** musical round 124 **while-ere** a while ago 125 **reason** anything within reason 127 **Flout ... 'em** insult them and mock them *tabor* small drum 133 **picture of Nobody** i.e. someone invisible 135 **take't ... list** take it as you will/do as you wish 143 **twangling** resonant/twanging 153 **by and by** soon/immediately 154 **story** scheme

STEPHANO Lead, monster: we'll follow. I would I could
    see this taborer: he lays it on.
TRINCULO Wilt come? I'll follow Stephano.   *To Caliban*

Exeunt

Act 3 Scene 3   *running scene 7*

Enter Alonso, Sebastian, Antonio, Gonzalo, Adrian,
Francisco and others

GONZALO By'r lakin, I can go no further, sir,
    My old bones ache. Here's a maze trod indeed
    Through forth-rights and meanders. By your
       patience,
    I needs must rest me.
5 ALONSO Old lord, I cannot blame thee,
    Who am myself attached with weariness
    To th'dulling of my spirits: sit down and rest.
    Even here I will put off my hope, and keep it
    No longer for my flatterer: he is drowned
10 Whom thus we stray to find, and the sea mocks
    Our frustrate search on land. Well, let him go.
    ANTONIO I am right glad that he's so out of hope.   *Aside to*
    Do not for one repulse forgo the purpose   *Sebastian*
    That you resolved t'effect.
15 SEBASTIAN The next advantage will we take thoroughly. *Aside to Antonio*
    ANTONIO Let it be tonight: *Aside to*
    For now they are oppressed with travail, they   *Sebastian*
    Will not, nor cannot use such vigilance
    As when they are fresh.
    Solemn and strange music: and [enter] Prospero on the top,
    invisible. Enter several strange shapes, bringing in a banquet,
    and dance about it with gentle actions of salutations, and
    inviting the king and others to eat, they depart
20 SEBASTIAN I say tonight: no more.   *Aside to Antonio*
    ALONSO What harmony is this? My good friends, hark!
    GONZALO Marvellous sweet music.
    ALONSO Give us kind keepers, heavens. What were
       these?

---

158 **taborer** drummer (i.e. Ariel)   **lays it on** i.e. bangs the drum with energy   **3.3   1 By'r lakin** by our
Ladykin (i.e. the Virgin Mary)   **2 maze** network of tracks, labyrinth   **3 forth-rights and meanders**
straight and winding paths   **6 attached** seized   **8 put off** cast off   **9 for my flatterer** to be my indulgent,
flattering courtier   **11 frustrate** fruitless/frustrated   **13 for** because of   **repulse** setback   **forgo** give up
17 oppressed worn down   **travail** labour/travelling   **23 keepers** protecting spirits

SEBASTIAN A living drollery. Now I will believe
25   That there are unicorns: that in Arabia
        There is one tree, the phoenix' throne, one phoenix
        At this hour reigning there.
ANTONIO I'll believe both:
        And what does else want credit, come to me,
30   And I'll be sworn 'tis true: travellers ne'er did lie,
        Though fools at home condemn 'em.
GONZALO If in Naples
        I should report this now, would they believe me?
        If I should say I saw such islanders —
35   For certes these are people of the island —
        Who though they are of monstrous shape, yet note
        Their manners are more gentle, kind, than of
        Our human generation you shall find
        Many, nay almost any.
40 **PROSPERO** Honest lord,   *Aside*
        Thou hast said well: for some of you there present
        Are worse than devils.
ALONSO I cannot too much muse
        Such shapes, such gesture, and such sound,
            expressing —
45   Although they want the use of tongue — a kind
        Of excellent dumb discourse.
PROSPERO Praise in departing.   *Aside*
FRANCISCO They vanished strangely.
SEBASTIAN No matter, since
50   They have left their viands behind: for we have
            stomachs.
        Will't please you taste of what is here?
ALONSO Not I.
GONZALO Faith, sir, you need not fear. When we were
            boys,
        Who would believe that there were mountaineers,
55   Dewlapped like bulls, whose throats had hanging
            at 'em
        Wallets of flesh? Or that there were such men
        Whose heads stood in their breasts? Which now
            we find

---

24 **drollery** puppet-show/comic entertainment/humorous picture   26 **phoenix** mythical Arabian bird that
was consumed by fire every 500 years, then resurrected from the ashes   29 **want credit** lack credibility
35 **certes** certainly   36 **monstrous** unnatural/unusual   38 **generation** race   43 **muse** wonder at
47 **Praise in departing** keep your praise until the occasion is over (proverbial)   48 **strangely** surprisingly/
unnaturally   50 **viands** food   **stomachs** appetites   54 **mountaineers** mountain dwellers
55 **Dewlapped** with folds of loose skin around the throat   56 **Wallets** sagging bags

Each putter-out of five for one will bring us
Good warrant of.

60 **ALONSO** I will stand to, and feed,
Although my last: no matter, since I feel
The best is past. Brother, my lord the duke,
Stand to, and do as we.

Thunder and lightning. Enter Ariel, like a harpy: claps his
wings upon the table, and, with a quaint device, the banquet
vanishes

ARIEL You are three men of sin, whom Destiny,
65 That hath to instrument this lower world
And what is in't, the never-surfeited sea
Hath caused to belch up you; and on this island,
Where man doth not inhabit — you 'mongst men
Being most unfit to live — I have made you mad;
70 And even with suchlike valour men hang and drown
Their proper selves. You fools: I and my fellows   *Alonso, Sebastian*
Are ministers of Fate: the elements   *and Antonio draw*
Of whom your swords are tempered may as well   *their swords*
Wound the loud winds, or with bemocked-at stabs
75 Kill the still-closing waters, as diminish
One dowl that's in my plume. My fellow ministers
Are like invulnerable. If you could hurt,
Your swords are now too massy for your strengths,
And will not be uplifted. But remember —
80 For that's my business to you — that you three
From Milan did supplant good Prospero,
Exposed unto the sea — which hath requit it —
Him and his innocent child: for which foul deed,
The powers, delaying — not forgetting — have
85 Incensed the seas and shores, yea, all the creatures
Against your peace. Thee of thy son, Alonso,
They have bereft: and do pronounce by me
Ling'ring perdition — worse than any death

---

58 putter-out … one brokers offered the traveller five times an initial sum deposited if he returned safely from his journey with proof that he had reached his destination   **putter-out** broker/traveller   **60 stand to** come forward/begin eating   **61 Although** even if (it is to be)   *harpy* mythical monster with a woman's face and body and a bird's wings and claws; sometimes agents of divine vengeance   *quaint device* ingenious mechanism/contrivance   **65 to instrument** at its disposal/as its agent   **lower world** i.e. the sub-lunar, mortal world   **66 never-surfeited** never satisfied, hungry   **70 suchlike valour** insane fearlessness
71 Their proper selves themselves   **72 elements … tempered** i.e. fire and earth from which your swords are forged (**tempered**); these two elements are powerless against the other two (**winds** and **waters**)
74 bemocked-at scorned   **75 still-closing** ever-united/self-healing   **76 dowl** small feather   **plume** plumage   **77 like** equally   **78 massy** heavy   **80 business** purpose   **82 requit** repaid/avenged
88 perdition ruin (with connotations of 'damnation')

Can be at once — shall step by step attend
90   You and your ways: whose wraths to guard you
          from,
       Which here in this most desolate isle else falls
       Upon your heads, is nothing but heart's sorrow
       And a clear life ensuing.
       He vanishes in thunder: then, to soft music, enter the shapes
       again, and dance, with mocks and mows, and carrying out
       the table [depart]
       PROSPERO Bravely the figure of this harpy hast thou
95   Performed, my Ariel: a grace it had, devouring:
           Of my instruction hast thou nothing bated
       In what thou hadst to say. So, with good life
       And observation strange, my meaner ministers
       Their several kinds have done. My high charms
          work,
100   And these, mine enemies, are all knit up
       In their distractions: they now are in my power,
       And in these fits I leave them, while I visit
       Young Ferdinand — whom they suppose is
          drowned —
       And his and mine loved darling.   [*Exit above*]
105   **GONZALO** I'th'name of something holy, sir, why stand
          you
       In this strange stare?
       ALONSO O, it is monstrous, monstrous:
       Methought the billows spoke and told me of it,
       The winds did sing it to me, and the thunder —
110   That deep and dreadful organ-pipe — pronounced
       The name of Prosper: it did bass my trespass.
       Therefore my son i'th'ooze is bedded: and
       I'll seek him deeper than e'er plummet sounded
       And with him there lie mudded.   *Exit*
115   **SEBASTIAN** But one fiend at a time,
       I'll fight their legions o'er.

---

90 whose … ensuing i.e. to guard yourselves from the anger of the **powers**, which will otherwise befall you on this deserted island, you must live a faultless life of profound repentance   *mocks and mows* jeering expressions/grimaces and pouts   **95 devouring** all-consuming (or possibly Ariel has eaten part of the banquet)   **96 bated** omitted   **97 So** likewise   **good life** great realism/much liveliness   **98 observation strange** particular, careful attention   **meaner** lower ranking   **99 several kinds** various/individual roles   **high** elevated, sophisticated, powerful   **100 knit up** tied up, entangled   **101 distractions** agitation, temporary madness   **102 fits** attacks, turmoil   **108 billows** great waves   **111 bass** pronounce in a deep, resonant voice   **trespass** wrong, crime   **112 i'th'ooze** in the muddy sand on the sea bed   **113 plummet** instrument used to measure the depth of water   **sounded** sank   **114 mudded** buried in mud   **115 But … o'er** as long as they come one at a time, I'll fight whole armies of devilish spirits

ANTONIO I'll be thy second. *Exeunt [Sebastian and Antonio]*
GONZALO All three of them are desperate: their great
     guilt,
Like poison given to work a great time after,
120   Now 'gins to bite the spirits. I do beseech you —
That are of suppler joints — follow them swiftly
And hinder them from what this ecstasy
May now provoke them to.
ADRIAN Follow, I pray you.   *Exeunt omnes*

Act 4 Scene 1   *running scene 8*

Enter Prospero, Ferdinand and Miranda

PROSPERO If I have too austerely punished you,   *To Ferdinand*
Your compensation makes amends, for I
Have given you here a third of mine own life,
Or that for which I live: who once again
5   I tender to thy hand. All thy vexations
Were but my trials of thy love, and thou
Hast strangely stood the test: here, afore heaven,
I ratify this my rich gift. O Ferdinand,
Do not smile at me that I boast her of,
10 For thou shalt find she will outstrip all praise
And make it halt behind her.
FERDINAND I do believe it gainst an oracle.
PROSPERO Then, as my guest, and thine own
     acquisition
Worthily purchased, take my daughter: but
15 If thou dost break her virgin-knot before
All sanctimonious ceremonies may
With full and holy rite be ministered,
No sweet aspersion shall the heavens let fall
To make this contract grow; but barren hate,
20 Sour-eyed disdain and discord shall bestrew
The union of your bed, with weeds so loathly

---

117 **second** supporter/back-up fighter in a duel   120 **spirits** faculties, vital powers   122 **ecstasy** frenzy
4.1   1 **austerely** severely   2 **compensation** i.e. Miranda   3 **third** i.e. a very important part (possibly
Miranda is a third of Prospero's age; or she shares his life with his dukedom and his art)   5 **tender** offer/
betroth   **vexations** afflictions   7 **strangely** admirably, exceptionally   8 **ratify** formally approve   9 **her of**
of her   11 **halt** proceed lamely   12 **gainst** even in the face of   14 **purchased** obtained/won
16 **sanctimonious** holy   18 **sweet aspersion** fragrant shower   20 **bestrew** cover   21 **loathly**
loathsome

That you shall hate it both. Therefore take heed,
As Hymen's lamps shall light you.

FERDINAND As I hope

25   For quiet days, fair issue and long life,
With such love as 'tis now, the murkiest den,
The most opportune place, the strong'st suggestion
Our worser genius can, shall never melt
Mine honour into lust, to take away

30   The edge of that day's celebration
When I shall think or Phoebus' steeds are foundered,
Or night kept chained below.

PROSPERO Fairly spoke.

Sit then and talk with her: she is thine own.   *Ferdinand and*

35   What, Ariel! My industrious servant, Ariel!   *Miranda sit and talk*

Enter Ariel

ARIEL What would my potent master? Here I am.

PROSPERO Thou and thy meaner fellows your last
      service
Did worthily perform, and I must use you
In such another trick. Go bring the rabble,

40   O'er whom I give thee power, here to this place:
Incite them to quick motion, for I must
Bestow upon the eyes of this young couple
Some vanity of mine art: it is my promise,
And they expect it from me.

45   **ARIEL** Presently?

PROSPERO Ay, with a twink.

ARIEL Before you can say 'come' and 'go',
And breathe twice and cry 'so, so',
Each one, tripping on his toe,

50   Will be here with mop and mow.
Do you love me, master? No?

PROSPERO Dearly, my delicate Ariel: do not approach
Till thou dost hear me call.

ARIEL Well: I conceive.   *Exit*

55   **PROSPERO** Look thou be true: do not give dalliance   *To Ferdinand*
Too much the rein: the strongest oaths are straw

---

23 **Hymen** in Greek and Roman mythology, the god of marriage (represented by a young man carrying a
lamp)   25 **fair issue** beautiful children   27 **strong'st … can** most powerful temptation/influence that our
bad angel (**worser genius**) can exert on us   31 **or** either   **Phoebus** the sun god, whose horse-drawn
chariot carried the sun across the heavens   **foundered** lame   39 **rabble** i.e. crowd of more lowly
spirits   43 **vanity** trifling/dazzling display   45 **Presently?** Immediately?   46 **with a twink** in the wink of
an eye   50 **mop and mow** grimace and pout   54 **conceive** understand   55 **true** faithful   **dalliance**
frivolity, amorous conversation

To th'fire i'th'blood: be more abstemious,
Or else goodnight your vow.

FERDINAND I warrant you, sir,
60   The white cold virgin snow upon my heart
Abates the ardour of my liver.

PROSPERO Well.
Now come, my Ariel! Bring a corollary,
Rather than want a spirit: appear, and pertly.
65   No tongue! All eyes! Be silent.

Soft music. Enter Iris

IRIS Ceres, most bounteous lady, thy rich leas
Of wheat, rye, barley, vetches, oats and peas;
Thy turfy mountains, where live nibbling sheep,
And flat meads thatched with stover, them to keep:
70   Thy banks with pionèd and twillèd brims,
Which spongy April at thy hest betrims
To make cold nymphs chaste crowns; and thy
    broom-groves,
Whose shadow the dismissèd bachelor loves,
Being lass-lorn: thy poll-clipped vineyard,
75   And thy sea-marge sterile and rocky-hard,
Where thou thyself dost air: the queen o'th'sky,
Whose wat'ry arch and messenger am I,
Bids thee leave these, and with her sovereign grace,

Juno descends   *In her chariot*

Here on this grass-plot, in this very place,
80   To come and sport. Her peacocks fly amain:
Approach, rich Ceres, her to entertain.

Enter Ceres

CERES Hail, many-coloured messenger, that ne'er
Dost disobey the wife of Jupiter:

---

57 **th'fire i'th'blood** passion, lust   58 **goodnight** farewell to   61 **liver** thought to be the seat of sexual desire   63 **a corollary** extra (spirits)   64 **pertly** briskly   *Iris* rainbow goddess and messenger of the gods   66 **Ceres** goddess of the harvest and the earth   **leas** fields   67 **vetches** coarse crops, often dried for animal feed   68 **turfy** grassy   69 **meads** meadows   **thatched with stover** covered with hay, winter animal feed   70 **pionèd ... brims** alluding to the agrarian practice of cutting and laying hedges to border or enclose pasture   **pionèd** dug, trenched   **twillèd** interwoven, plaited branches   **brims** hedges, borders   71 **spongy** rainy, damp   **hest** command   **betrims** trims with dew or rain/adorns with blossom   72 **cold** modest, chaste   **crowns** coronets of flowers   **broom-groves** groves of broom (a yellow-flowered shrub)   73 **dismissèd** rejected   74 **lass-lorn** forsaken, bereft of a sweetheart   **poll-clipped** pollarded, pruned   75 **sea-marge** coast   76 **air** take the air   **queen o'th'sky** i.e. Juno   77 **wat'ry arch** rainbow   78 **these** i.e. the landscape described above   80 **sport** make merry   **peacocks** the sacred birds of Juno who drew her carriage   **amain** swiftly   83 **wife of Jupiter** Juno, married to the king of the gods

Who, with thy saffron wings, upon my flowers
85   Diffusest honey drops, refreshing showers,
And with each end of thy blue bow dost crown
My bosky acres and my unshrubbed down,
Rich scarf to my proud earth: why hath thy queen
Summoned me hither to this short-grassed green?
90   **IRIS** A contract of true love to celebrate,
And some donation freely to estate
On the blest lovers.
     CERES Tell me, heavenly bow,
If Venus or her son, as thou dost know,
95   Do now attend the queen? Since they did plot
The means that dusky Dis my daughter got,
Her and her blind boy's scandaled company
I have forsworn.
     IRIS Of her society
100   Be not afraid: I met her deity
Cutting the clouds towards Paphos, and her son
Dove-drawn with her. Here thought they to have
   done
Some wanton charm upon this man and maid,
Whose vows are that no bed-right shall be paid
105   Till Hymen's torch be lighted — but in vain.
Mars' hot minion is returned again:
Her waspish-headed son has broke his arrows,
Swears he will shoot no more, but play with
   sparrows,
And be a boy right out.
110   **CERES** Highest queen of state,
Great Juno, comes: I know her by her gait.   *Juno alights*
     JUNO How does my bounteous sister? Go with me
To bless this twain, that they may prosperous be,
And honoured in their issue.

---

84 **saffron** orange-red   85 **Diffusest honey drops** scatters sweet rain/dew   86 **bow** rainbow   87 **bosky** bushy, full of thickets   **unshrubbed down** bare, undulating hills   88 **proud** splendid   91 **donation** gift, favour   **estate** bestow   94 **Venus … son** Cupid was son to Venus, goddess of love   96 **means that** manner in which   **dusky Dis** dark Pluto, the rich god of the underworld; aided by Venus and Cupid, he kidnapped Ceres' daughter Proserpine who was forced to spend half of every year with him   97 **blind boy's** Cupid, god of love, was blind   **scandaled** disgraceful   98 **forsworn** rejected   101 **Paphos** city in Cyprus, home to the cult of Venus   102 **Dove-drawn** doves, the birds of love, pull Venus' chariot   103 **wanton** mischievous/lascivious   104 **bed-right** i.e. sex   105 **Hymen's … lighted** symbolizing the completion of the marriage ceremony   106 **Mars' hot minion** i.e. lustful Venus, lover to the god of war   107 **waspish-headed** peevish, spiteful and, literally, one who stings (with **arrows**)   108 **sparrows** proverbially lecherous birds   109 **be … out** behave in all respects like a boy not a god   111 **gait** bearing, movement   112 **bounteous** generous   113 **twain** couple

115	JUNO Honour, riches, marriage-blessing,	*They sing*
	Long continuance, and increasing,	
	Hourly joys be still upon you,	
	Juno sings her blessings on you.	

CERES Earth's increase, foison plenty,
120   Barns and garners never empty,
         Vines with clust'ring bunches growing,
         Plants with goodly burden bowing:
         Spring come to you at the farthest,
         In the very end of harvest.
125   Scarcity and want shall shun you,
         Ceres' blessing so is on you.

FERDINAND This is a most majestic vision, and
         Harmonious charmingly. May I be bold
         To think these spirits?

130 PROSPERO Spirits, which by mine art
         I have from their confines called to enact
         My present fancies.

FERDINAND Let me live here ever:
         So rare a wondered father, and a wise,
135   Makes this place paradise.

PROSPERO Sweet, now, silence!
         Juno and Ceres whisper seriously:
         There's something else to do. Hush, and be mute,
         Or else our spell is marred.

Juno and Ceres whisper, and send Iris on employment

140 IRIS You nymphs, called Naiads, of the windring brooks,
         With your sedged crowns and ever-harmless looks,
         Leave your crisp channels, and on this green land
         Answer your summons: Juno does command.
         Come, temperate nymphs, and help to celebrate
145   A contract of true love: be not too late.

Enter certain nymphs

         You sunburned sicklemen of August weary,
         Come hither from the furrow and be merry:
         Make holiday: your rye-straw hats put on,

---

116 **increasing** children/fruitfulness   117 **still** always   119 **foison** abundance   120 **garners** granaries
123 **Spring** … **harvest** may spring arrive as soon as the autumn harvest is over (so there is no winter)
128 **charmingly** enchantingly/melodiously/pleasingly   **be bold** take the liberty, venture   132 **present fancies** immediate imaginings/whims   134 **wondered** to be wondered at, extraordinary   137 **seriously** importantly/solemnly   140 **Naiads** water nymphs   **windring** winding and wandering   141 **sedged** made from sedge, a coarse grassy plant growing by rivers   142 **crisp channels** rippling streams
144 **temperate** gentle/abstemious   145 **be** … **late** come quickly/arrive before the couple make love
146 **sicklemen** harvesters (a sickle is a hooked knife used for reaping)   147 **furrow** i.e. fields (literally, groove made by a plough)

And these fresh nymphs encounter every one
150   In country footing.

Enter certain reapers, properly habited: they join with the
nymphs in a graceful dance, towards the end whereof
Prospero starts suddenly and speaks: after which, to a
strange, hollow, and confused noise, they heavily vanish

PROSPERO I had forgot that foul conspiracy   *Aside*
     Of the beast Caliban and his confederates
     Against my life: the minute of their plot
     Is almost come.— Well done. Avoid: no more!   *To the spirits*
155 FERDINAND This is strange: your father's in some passion   *To Miranda*
     That works him strongly.

MIRANDA Never till this day
     Saw I him touched with anger, so distempered.

PROSPERO You do look, my son, in a movèd sort,
160   As if you were dismayed: be cheerful, sir.
     Our revels now are ended. These our actors,
     As I foretold you, were all spirits and
     Are melted into air, into thin air,
     And, like the baseless fabric of this vision,
165   The cloud-capped towers, the gorgeous palaces,
     The solemn temples, the great Globe itself,
     Yea, all which it inherit, shall dissolve,
     And, like this insubstantial pageant faded,
     Leave not a rack behind. We are such stuff
170   As dreams are made on; and our little life
     Is rounded with a sleep. Sir, I am vexed,
     Bear with my weakness, my old brain is troubled:
     Be not disturbed with my infirmity.
     If you be pleased, retire into my cell
175   And there repose. A turn or two I'll walk
     To still my beating mind.

FERDINAND *and* MIRANDA   We wish your peace.
                    Exeunt [Ferdinand and Miranda]

PROSPERO Come with a thought: I thank thee, Ariel:
        come!

Enter Ariel

---

150 **country footing** rustic dance   *properly habited* appropriately clad (i.e. in their harvesting clothes)
heavily slowly, sadly/suddenly   154 **Avoid** be gone   155 **passion** agitation, turmoil   158 **distempered**
disturbed, ill-humoured   159 **movèd sort** distressed state   161 **revels** (courtly) entertainment/masque
162 **foretold you** told you earlier   164 **baseless** without a foundation/illusory   **fabric** building/structure
166 **Globe** world (puns on the Globe theatre)   167 **all** i.e. all those, all the people   **it** i.e. the **globe**
168 **pageant** spectacle/scene   169 **rack** shred of cloud, fragment of mist (perhaps with play on 'wrack' –
i.e. wreck)   171 **rounded** completed/surrounded (perhaps with play on 'crowned')   174 **cell** humble
dwelling   178 **with a thought** quickly, as swiftly as I think of you

ARIEL Thy thoughts I cleave to: what's thy pleasure?
180 **PROSPERO** Spirit, we must prepare to meet with Caliban.
ARIEL Ay, my commander: when I presented Ceres,
    I thought to have told thee of it, but I feared
    Lest I might anger thee.
PROSPERO Say again, where didst thou leave these
    varlets?
185 **ARIEL** I told you, sir, they were red-hot with drinking,
    So full of valour that they smote the air
    For breathing in their faces, beat the ground
    For kissing of their feet: yet always bending
    Towards their project. Then I beat my tabor,
190   At which, like unbacked colts, they pricked
      their ears,
    Advanced their eyelids, lifted up their noses
    As they smelt music: so I charmed their ears,
    That calf-like they my lowing followed through
    Toothed briars, sharp furzes, pricking gorse
      and thorns,
195   Which entered their frail shins: at last I left them
    I'th'filthy-mantled pool beyond your cell,
    There dancing up to th'chins, that the foul lake
    O'erstunk their feet.
PROSPERO This was well done, my bird.
200   Thy shape invisible retain thou still:
    The trumpery in my house, go bring it hither,
    For stale to catch these thieves.
ARIEL I go, I go.   *Exit*
PROSPERO A devil, a born devil, on whose nature
205   Nurture can never stick: on whom my pains,
    Humanely taken, all, all lost, quite lost.
    And as with age his body uglier grows,
    So his mind cankers. I will plague them all,
    Even to roaring. Come, hang them on this line.
Enter Ariel, loaden with glistering apparel etc.   **Ariel hangs up the finery**

---

179 **cleave to** adhere to, respond rapidly to   184 **varlets** rogues   185 **red-hot** fired up/red in the face
186 **smote** struck   188 **bending** turning, proceeding   190 **unbacked colts** untrained, unbroken
young horses   191 **Advanced** opened   192 **As** as if   193 **lowing** mooing   194 **Toothed** prickly
briars ... thorns all types of thorny, coarse shrubs   196 **filthy-mantled** covered with scum or rotting
weeds   197 **that** so that   **lake ... feet** i.e. being stirred up, the lake stank even more foully than their feet
200 **Thy ... still** i.e. remain invisible   201 **trumpery** fancy garments, worthless finery   202 **stale** bait
206 **Humanely** as a human/benevolently   **lost** wasted on him/corrupted by him   208 **cankers** decays,
becomes malignant   209 **roaring** moaning, wailing   **line** clothes-line/lind (i.e. lime tree)   *glistering*
glittering

Enter Caliban, Stephano and Trinculo, all wet   *Prospero and Ariel*
                                                    stand apart

210 **CALIBAN** Pray you, tread softly, that the blind mole may
        not hear a footfall: we now are near his cell.
    STEPHANO Monster, your fairy, which you say is a
        harmless fairy, has done little better than played the
        jack with us.
215 **TRINCULO** Monster, I do smell all horse-piss, at which my
        nose is in great indignation.
    STEPHANO So is mine. Do you hear, monster? If I should
        take a displeasure against you, look you—
    TRINCULO Thou wert but a lost monster.
220 **CALIBAN** Good my lord, give me thy favour still.
        Be patient, for the prize I'll bring thee to
        Shall hoodwink this mischance: therefore speak
            softly,
        All's hushed as midnight yet.
    TRINCULO Ay, but to lose our bottles in the pool!
225 **STEPHANO** There is not only disgrace and dishonour in
        that, monster, but an infinite loss.
    TRINCULO That's more to me than my wetting: yet this is
        your harmless fairy, monster.
    STEPHANO I will fetch off my bottle, though I be o'er ears
230   for my labour.
    CALIBAN Prithee, my king, be quiet. See'st thou here,
        This is the mouth o'th'cell: no noise, and enter.
        Do that good mischief which may make this island
        Thine own forever, and I thy Caliban
235   For aye thy foot-licker.
    STEPHANO Give me thy hand. I do begin to have bloody
        thoughts.
    TRINCULO O King Stephano, O peer! O worthy
        Stephano, look what a wardrobe here is for thee!   *Sees the apparel*
240 **CALIBAN** Let it alone, thou fool: it is but trash.
    TRINCULO O, ho, monster: we know what belongs to a
        frippery. O King Stephano!   *Puts on a gown*
    STEPHANO Put off that gown, Trinculo: by this hand, I'll
        have that gown.
245 **TRINCULO** Thy grace shall have it.

---

210 **that** so that even   212 **fairy** i.e. Ariel   213 **played … with** tricked/played the knave   219 **lost**
ruined, destitute   222 **hoodwink this mischance** cover up this misfortune   229 **fetch off** retrieve   **o'er**
ears up to my ears (in the stinking lake)   233 **mischief** evil, wrongdoing   235 **aye** ever   238 **King …**
peer allusion to a popular ballad ('King Stephen was a worthy peer') about kings and their clothing
242 **frippery** second-hand clothes shop

CALIBAN The dropsy drown this fool: what do you mean
To dote thus on such luggage? Let's alone
And do the murder first: if he awake,
From toe to crown he'll fill our skins with pinches,
250   Make us strange stuff.

STEPHANO Be you quiet, monster.— Mistress line, is not
this my jerkin? Now is the jerkin under the line: now,   *Takes it down*
jerkin, you are like to lose your hair and prove a bald
jerkin.

255   **TRINCULO** Do, do: we steal by line and level, an't like
your grace.

STEPHANO I thank thee for that jest: here's a garment   *Gives Trinculo a*
for't: wit shall not go unrewarded while I am king of   *garment*
this country. 'Steal by line and level' is an excellent
260   pass of pate: there's another garment for't.   *Gives another*

TRINCULO Monster, come put some lime upon your
fingers, and away with the rest.

CALIBAN I will have none on't: we shall lose our time,
And all be turned to barnacles, or to apes
265   With foreheads villainous low.

STEPHANO Monster, lay to your fingers: help to bear this
away where my hogshead of wine is, or I'll turn you
out of my kingdom: go to, carry this.

TRINCULO And this.   *They load Caliban*
270   **STEPHANO** Ay, and this.   *with garments*

A noise of hunters heard. Enter diverse spirits, in shape of
dogs and hounds, hunting them about, Prospero and Ariel
setting them on

PROSPERO Hey, Mountain, hey!

ARIEL Silver! There it goes, Silver!

PROSPERO Fury, Fury! There, Tyrant, there: hark!   *Caliban, Stephano*
hark!   *and Trinculo are driven out*
Go, charge my goblins that they grind their joints   *To Ariel*
275   With dry convulsions, shorten up their sinews

---

246 dropsy disease in which the body accumulates fluid   **247 luggage** trappings, encumbrances
250 Make … stuff transform us into extraordinary material   **251 Mistress line** i.e. the clothes-line/tree
252 jerkin close-fitting jacket   **under the line** off the clothes-line or tree/at the equator, or metaphorically,
genitals, and thus **bald** from either a sailor's fever or syphilis   **253 hair** many jerkins were made from animal
fur and cured (i.e. 'hairless') leather   **255 by … level** methodically   **an't like** if it please   **260 pass of
pate** witty thrust   **261 lime** birdlime, a sticky substance spread on branches to snare birds   **264 barnacles**
sea creatures/type of goose (hence connotations of stupidity, as with **apes**)   **265 villainous** villainously/
vilely (playing on 'villain', a servant or lowly person)   **266 lay to your** use   **267 hogshead** large cask
diverse various   **271 Mountain … Tyrant** the names of the spirits as hounds, all of which imply their
powerful personalities   **274 grind** torment/crush   **275 dry convulsions** painful cramps   **shorten up**
contract

With agèd cramps, and more pinch-spotted
  make them
Than pard or cat o'mountain.

ARIEL Hark, they roar.

PROSPERO Let them be hunted soundly. At this hour
280   Lies at my mercy all mine enemies:
Shortly shall all my labours end, and thou
Shalt have the air at freedom: for a little,
Follow, and do me service.   *Exeunt*

Act 5 Scene 1

running scene 9

Enter Prospero in his magic robes, and Ariel

PROSPERO Now does my project gather to a head.
My charms crack not, my spirits obey, and Time
Goes upright with his carriage. How's the day?

ARIEL On the sixth hour, at which time, my lord,
5   You said our work should cease.

PROSPERO I did say so,
When first I raised the tempest. Say, my spirit,
How fares the king and's followers?

ARIEL Confined together
10   In the same fashion as you gave in charge,
Just as you left them; all prisoners, sir,
In the line-grove which weather-fends your cell:
They cannot budge till your release. The king,
His brother, and yours abide all three distracted,
15   And the remainder mourning over them,
Brimful of sorrow and dismay: but chiefly
Him that you termed, sir, the good old lord Gonzalo:
His tears run down his beard, like winter's drops
From eaves of reeds. Your charm so strongly
  works 'em
20   That if you now beheld them, your affections
Would become tender.

PROSPERO Dost thou think so, spirit?

ARIEL Mine would, sir, were I human.

---

276 **agèd cramps** pains of old age   **pinch-spotted** bruised from pinches   277 **pard** leopard/panther
cat o'mountain wild cat   282 **air at freedom** freedom of the air (i.e. be released)   **little** short time
5.1   1 project plan (with associations of 'alchemical experiment')   **gather ... head** come to fruition/begin
to boil (a vital stage in alchemy)   **2 crack not** do not fail/do not overboil   **Time ... carriage** Time walks
more easily with his burden   **3 How's the day?** What time is it?   **10 gave in charge** instructed   **12 line-
grove** grove of lime trees   **weather-fends** shelters   **14 abide** remain   **distracted** distressed/maddened
17 termed called   **18 winter's ... reeds** winter rain from thatched roofs   **20 affections** feelings

PROSPERO And mine shall.

25 Hast thou, which art but air, a touch, a feeling
Of their afflictions, and shall not myself,
One of their kind, that relish all as sharply
Passion as they, be kindlier moved than thou art?
Though with their high wrongs I am struck to
th'quick,

30 Yet with my nobler reason gainst my fury
Do I take part: the rarer action is
In virtue than in vengeance. They being penitent,
The sole drift of my purpose doth extend
Not a frown further. Go, release them, Ariel:

35 My charms I'll break, their senses I'll restore,
And they shall be themselves.

ARIEL I'll fetch them, sir.   *Exit*

PROSPERO Ye elves of hills, brooks, standing lakes
and groves,
And ye that on the sands with printless foot

40 Do chase the ebbing Neptune, and do fly him
When he comes back: you demi-puppets that
By moonshine do the green sour ringlets make,
Whereof the ewe not bites: and you whose pastime
Is to make midnight mushrooms, that rejoice

45 To hear the solemn curfew, by whose aid —
Weak masters though ye be — I have bedimmed
The noontide sun, called forth the mutinous winds,
And 'twixt the green sea and the azured vault
Set roaring war: to the dread rattling thunder

50 Have I given fire, and rifted Jove's stout oak
With his own bolt: the strong-based promontory
Have I made shake and by the spurs plucked up
The pine and cedar. Graves at my command
Have waked their sleepers, oped, and let 'em forth

55 By my so potent art. But this rough magic   *Prospero traces*
I here abjure: and when I have required   *a circle with his staff*

27 **relish ... Passion** feel the force of emotion/suffering as acutely   28 **kindlier moved** affected with more
compassion   29 **high** extreme   **th'quick** the most tender part   31 **take part** join forces   **rarer** more
unusual/profound   32 **than** rather than   33 **drift** aim   38 **standing** still/stagnant   39 **with printless
foot** leaving no trace   40 **fly** flee   41 **demi-puppets** tiny creatures   42 **ringlets** fairy rings, darker circles
of grass supposedly caused by fairies dancing   43 **ewe not bites** sheep will not eat the grass because it is
sour   44 **midnight mushrooms** mushrooms that grow overnight; toadstools were particularly associated
with fairies   45 **solemn curfew** nine o'clock bell; after the evening curfew, the spirits were free until dawn
46 **masters** ministers/magicians   **bedimmed** eclipsed/clouded over   48 **azured vault** blue sky
49 **Set roaring war** i.e. caused a storm   50 **fire** i.e. lightning   **rifted** split   **oak** a tree particularly
associated with the king of the gods   51 **strong-based promontory** sturdy headland   52 **spurs** i.e. roots
54 **oped** opened   55 **rough** violent/imperfect   56 **abjure** solemnly reject   **required** summoned

Some heavenly music — which even now I do —
To work mine end upon their senses that
This airy charm is for, I'll break my staff,
60   Bury it certain fathoms in the earth,
And deeper than did ever plummet sound
I'll drown my book.

Solemn music. Here enters Ariel before: then Alonso, with a
frantic gesture, attended by Gonzalo: Sebastian and Antonio
in like manner, attended by Adrian and Francisco. They all
enter the circle which Prospero had made, and there stand
charmed: which Prospero observing, speaks:

A solemn air, and the best comforter   *To Alonso*
To an unsettled fancy, cure thy brains,
65   Now useless, boil within thy skull!— There stand,   *To Sebastian*
For you are spell-stopped.   *and Antonio*
Holy Gonzalo, honourable man,   *To Gonzalo*
Mine eyes, ev'n sociable to the show of thine,
Fall fellowly drops.— The charm dissolves apace,   *Aside*
70   And as the morning steals upon the night,
Melting the darkness, so their rising senses
Begin to chase the ignorant fumes that mantle
Their clearer reason.— O good Gonzalo,
My true preserver, and a loyal sir
75   To him thou follow'st, I will pay thy graces
Home both in word and deed.— Most cruelly
Didst thou, Alonso, use me and my daughter:
Thy brother was a furtherer in the act.—
Thou art pinched for't now, Sebastian.—
Flesh and blood,   *To Antonio*
80   You, brother mine, that entertain ambition,
Expelled remorse and nature: whom, with
Sebastian —
Whose inward pinches therefore are most strong —
Would here have killed your king: I do forgive thee,
Unnatural though thou art. Their understanding
85   Begins to swell, and the approaching tide
Will shortly fill the reasonable shore

---

58 end purpose   60 certain a certain number of   fathoms a fathom was about six feet   61 plummet
instrument used to measure the depth of water   sound penetrate   *frantic* mad   63 air melody   64 fancy
imagination   65 boil that boil   66 spell-stopped motionless, arrested by the spell   68 sociable
sympathetic   show sight (Gonzalo is weeping)   69 Fall fellowly let fall compassionate   apace swiftly
71 rising awakening   72 ignorant dull/befuddled   mantle cloak   74 true honest   75 follow'st serve
pay ... Home repay the debt in full   78 furtherer enabler   80 entertain court/welcome   81 remorse
and nature pity and kinship   82 inward pinches inner turmoil/tortures of conscience   85 the ... shore
i.e. their awakening senses begin to move them towards understanding

That now lies foul and muddy. Not one of them
That yet looks on me or would know me. Ariel,
Fetch me the hat and rapier in my cell:

90   I will discase me, and myself present
As I was sometime Milan. Quickly, spirit: *Ariel gets hat and rapier,*
Thou shalt ere long be free.   *returns immediately*
Ariel sings and helps to attire him:
ARIEL Where the bee sucks, there suck I:
    In a cowslip's bell I lie:

95   There I couch when owls do cry.
    On the bat's back I do fly
    After summer merrily.
    Merrily, merrily shall I live now
    Under the blossom that hangs on the bough.

100 **PROSPERO** Why, that's my dainty Ariel. I shall miss
Thee: but yet thou shalt have freedom. So, so, so. *Arranges his attire*
To the king's ship, invisible as thou art:
There shalt thou find the mariners asleep
Under the hatches: the master and the boatswain

105   Being awake, enforce them to this place;
And presently, I prithee.
ARIEL I drink the air before me, and return
Or ere your pulse twice beat.   *Exit*
GONZALO All torment, trouble, wonder, and amazement

110   Inhabits here: some heavenly power guide us
Out of this fearful country!
PROSPERO Behold, sir king,
The wrongèd Duke of Milan, Prospero:
For more assurance that a living prince

115   Does now speak to thee, I embrace thy body,
And to thee and thy company, I bid   *Embraces him*
A hearty welcome.
ALONSO Whether thou be'st he or no,
Or some enchanted trifle to abuse me —

120   As late I have been — I not know: thy pulse
Beats as of flesh and blood: and since I saw thee
Th'affliction of my mind amends, with which
I fear a madness held me: this must crave —
An if this be at all — a most strange story.

89 **hat and rapier** signs of a gentleman   **rapier** sword   90 **discase me** undress/change costume
91 **As … Milan** as I looked when I was Duke of Milan   94 **cowslip's bell** the bell-shaped petals that form
the flower   95 **couch** rest/conceal myself   105 **enforce** urge/drive   106 **presently** immediately
107 **drink the air** i.e. devour the way, travel quickly   108 **Or ere** before   111 **fearful** terrifying/awe-
inspiring   119 **trifle** illusion, trick   **abuse** deceive/harm   122 **amends** improves   124 **be at all** is even
real

125   Thy dukedom I resign, and do entreat
    Thou pardon me my wrongs. But how should Prospero
    Be living and be here?

PROSPERO First, noble friend,   *To Gonzalo*
    Let me embrace thine age, whose honour cannot
130   Be measured or confined.

GONZALO Whether this be
    Or be not, I'll not swear.

PROSPERO You do yet taste
    Some subtleties o'th'isle, that will not let you
135   Believe things certain. Welcome, my friends all.—
    But you, my brace of lords, were I so minded,   *Aside to*
    I here could pluck his highness' frown upon you,   *Sebastian and*
    And justify you traitors: at this time,   *Antonio*
    I will tell no tales.
140 **SEBASTIAN** The devil speaks in him.   *Aside to Antonio,*
                                               but overheard by Prospero

PROSPERO No.—
    For you, most wicked sir, whom to call brother   *To Antonio*
    Would even infect my mouth, I do forgive
    Thy rankest fault — all of them — and require
145   My dukedom of thee, which perforce I know
    Thou must restore.

ALONSO If thou be'st Prospero,
    Give us particulars of thy preservation:
    How thou hast met us here, whom three hours since
150   Were wrecked upon this shore? Where I have lost —
    How sharp the point of this remembrance is —
    My dear son Ferdinand.

PROSPERO I am woe for't, sir.

ALONSO Irreparable is the loss, and Patience
155   Says it is past her cure.

PROSPERO I rather think
    You have not sought her help, of whose soft grace
    For the like loss, I have her sovereign aid,
    And rest myself content.
160 **ALONSO** You the like loss?

PROSPERO As great to me as late, and supportable
    To make the dear loss have I means much weaker

---

125 **Thy ... resign** Alonso gives up his claims over Milan, a tributary state to Naples   131 **be ... not** is or is not real   134 **subtleties** illusions, magical contrivances (plays on sense of 'sugar confections')   136 **brace** pair   138 **you** you as   144 **rankest** most grievous   145 **perforce** of necessity   153 **woe** sorry   158 **the like** a similar   **sovereign** excellent/healing   159 **content** satisfied/resigned   161 **late** recent **supportable ... weaker** I have far fewer means at my disposal with which to make my grief bearable

Than you may call to comfort you: for I
Have lost my daughter.

165 **ALONSO** A daughter?
O heavens, that they were living both in Naples,
The king and queen there! That they were, I wish
Myself were mudded in that oozy bed
Where my son lies. When did you lose your
daughter?

170 **PROSPERO** In this last tempest. I perceive these lords
At this encounter do so much admire
That they devour their reason and scarce think
Their eyes do offices of truth: their words
Are natural breath. But, howsoe'er you have

175 Been justled from your senses, know for certain
That I am Prospero, and that very duke
Which was thrust forth of Milan, who most strangely
Upon this shore, where you were wrecked, was
landed
To be the lord on't. No more yet of this,

180 For 'tis a chronicle of day by day,
Not a relation for a breakfast, nor
Befitting this first meeting. Welcome, sir:
This cell's my court: here have I few attendants,
And subjects none abroad: pray you look in.

185 My dukedom since you have given me again,
I will requite you with as good a thing,
At least bring forth a wonder, to content ye
As much as me my dukedom.

*Here Prospero discovers Ferdinand and Miranda playing at
chess*

MIRANDA Sweet lord, you play me false.

190 **FERDINAND** No, my dearest love,
I would not for the world.

MIRANDA Yes, for a score of kingdoms you should
wrangle,
And I would call it fair play.

ALONSO If this prove

195 A vision of the island, one dear son
Shall I twice lose.

---

167 That they were i.e. were it necessary in order for that to be the case   **171 do ... admire** are so
astonished   **172 they ... reason** their reason is consumed   **think ... truth** believe their eyes
173 their ... breath they are speechless   **175 justled** jostled   **179 on't** of it   **180 chronicle ... day**
narrative to be told over many days/one day at a time   **181 relation** report   **184 abroad** elsewhere
186 requite repay/respond to   **187 wonder** puns on Miranda's name   **189 play me false** are cheating
192 a score twenty   **wrangle** wage war

SEBASTIAN A most high miracle.

FERDINAND Though the seas threaten, they are merciful:
I have cursed them without cause.   *Kneels*

200 ALONSO Now all the blessings
Of a glad father compass thee about.
Arise, and say how thou cam'st here.

MIRANDA O wonder!
How many goodly creatures are there here!
205 How beauteous mankind is! O brave new world,
That has such people in't.

PROSPERO 'Tis new to thee.

ALONSO What is this maid with whom thou wast at   *To Ferdinand*
play?
Your eld'st acquaintance cannot be three hours:
210 Is she the goddess that hath severed us,
And brought us thus together?

FERDINAND Sir, she is mortal:
But by immortal providence, she's mine:
I chose her when I could not ask my father
215 For his advice, nor thought I had one. She
Is daughter to this famous Duke of Milan,
Of whom so often I have heard renown,
But never saw before: of whom I have
Received a second life: and second father
220 This lady makes him to me.

ALONSO I am hers.
But, O, how oddly will it sound that I
Must ask my child forgiveness.

PROSPERO There sir, stop:
225 Let us not burden our remembrances with
A heaviness that's gone.

GONZALO I have inly wept,
Or should have spoke ere this. Look down you gods,
And on this couple drop a blessèd crown.
230 For it is you that have chalked forth the way
Which brought us hither.

ALONSO I say amen, Gonzalo.

GONZALO Was Milan thrust from Milan that his issue
Should become kings of Naples? O, rejoice
235 Beyond a common joy, and set it down

197 **miracle** continues wordplay on Miranda's name   201 **compass** encircle   204 **goodly** splendid,
worthy   209 **eld'st** oldest, longest   215 **one** i.e. a living father   217 **renown** report/honour   221 **hers**
i.e. her father (in-law)   226 **heaviness** grief/weight   227 **inly** inwardly   230 **chalked forth** marked out
233 **Milan ... Milan** i.e. the Duke of Milan (Prospero) ... the dukedom

With gold on lasting pillars: in one voyage
Did Claribel her husband find at Tunis,
And Ferdinand her brother found a wife
Where he himself was lost, Prospero his dukedom
240   In a poor isle, and all of us our selves
When no man was his own.

ALONSO Give me your hands: *To Ferdinand*
Let grief and sorrow still embrace his heart   *and Miranda*
That doth not wish you joy.

245   GONZALO Be it so. Amen!
Enter Ariel, with the Master and Boatswain amazedly
following
O, look, sir, look, sir! Here is more of us!
I prophesied, if a gallows were on land,
This fellow could not drown.— Now, blasphemy,   *To Boatswain*
That swear'st grace o'erboard, not an oath on shore?
250   Hast thou no mouth by land? What is the news?

BOATSWAIN The best news is that we have safely found
Our king and company: the next, our ship,
Which but three glasses since we gave out split,
Is tight and yare and bravely rigged as when
255   We first put out to sea.

ARIEL Sir, all this service   *Aside to Prospero*
Have I done since I went.

PROSPERO My tricksy spirit!   *Aside to Ariel*

ALONSO These are not natural events: they strengthen
260   From strange to stranger. Say, how came you hither?

BOATSWAIN If I did think, sir, I were well awake,
I'd strive to tell you. We were dead of sleep,
And — how we know not — all clapped under
  hatches,
Where, but even now, with strange and several
  noises
265   Of roaring, shrieking, howling, jingling chains,
And more diversity of sounds, all horrible,
We were awaked: straightway at liberty,
Where we, in all our trim, freshly beheld
Our royal, good and gallant ship, our master
270   Cap'ring to eye her. On a trice, so please you,

---

243 still always   **his heart That** the heart of anyone who   **248 blasphemy** ... **shore** i.e. the Boatswain,
who curses freely on his ship, is uncharacteristically silent   **253 glasses** hourglasses (i.e. three hours)
gave out reported   **254 tight and yare** efficient and seaworthy   **258 tricksy** cleverly playful
263 clapped under hatches shut up below deck   **264 several** various   **267 at liberty** i.e. released from
below deck   **268 trim** finery/clothes   **270 Cap'ring** leaping/dancing   **On a trice** instantly

Even in a dream, were we divided from them
And were brought moping hither.

ARIEL Was't well done?   *Aside to Prospero*

PROSPERO Bravely, my diligence. Thou shalt be free.   *Aside to Ariel*

275 **ALONSO** This is as strange a maze as e'er men trod,
And there is in this business more than nature
Was ever conduct of: some oracle
Must rectify our knowledge.

PROSPERO Sir, my liege,
280 Do not infest your mind with beating on
The strangeness of this business. At picked leisure —
Which shall be shortly single — I'll resolve you,
Which to you shall seem probable, of every
These happened accidents. Till when, be cheerful
285 And think of each thing well.— Come hither, spirit,   *Aside to Ariel*
Set Caliban and his companions free:
Untie the spell.—   [*Exit Ariel*]
                  How fares my gracious sir?   *To Alonso*
There are yet missing of your company
Some few odd lads that you remember not.

*Enter Ariel, driving in Caliban, Stephano and Trinculo, in
their stolen apparel*

290 **STEPHANO** Every man shift for all the rest, and let no
man take care for himself: for all is but fortune.
Coraggio, bully-monster, *coraggio*!

TRINCULO If these be true spies which I wear in my head,
here's a goodly sight.

295 **CALIBAN** O Setebos, these be brave spirits indeed!
How fine my master is! I am afraid
He will chastise me.

SEBASTIAN Ha, ha!
What things are these, my lord Antonio?
300 Will money buy 'em?

ANTONIO Very like. One of them
Is a plain fish, and no doubt marketable.

PROSPERO Mark but the badges of these men, my lords,
Then say if they be true. This misshapen knave,
305 His mother was a witch, and one so strong

---

272 **moping** dazed, bewildered   277 **conduct** guide/director   280 **beating** dwelling   281 **picked leisure** a chosen moment of free time   282 **be shortly single** soon be undivided (referring to leisure)   283 **Which ... probable** in a manner that will convince you   284 **happened accidents** events that have taken place   285 **well** easily/cheerfully   290 **shift** look out   291 **fortune** chance, fate   *Coraggio* 'have courage' (Italian)   292 **bully** gallant/my old mate   293 **spies** i.e. eyes   301 **like** likely   **One ... fish** presumably Caliban   303 **badges** livery   304 **true** legitimate/honest

That could control the moon, make flows and ebbs,
And deal in her command without her power:
These three have robbed me, and this demi-devil —
For he's a bastard one — had plotted with them
310   To take my life. Two of these fellows you
Must know and own: this thing of darkness I
Acknowledge mine.

CALIBAN I shall be pinched to death.

ALONSO Is not this Stephano, my drunken butler?

315 **SEBASTIAN** He is drunk now: where had he wine?

ALONSO And Trinculo is reeling ripe: where should they
Find this grand liquor that hath gilded 'em?
How cam'st thou in this pickle?   *To Trinculo*

TRINCULO I have been in such a pickle since I saw you
320   last that I fear me will never out of my bones: I shall
not fear fly-blowing.

SEBASTIAN Why, how now, Stephano?

STEPHANO O, touch me not: I am not Stephano, but a
cramp.

325 **PROSPERO** You'd be king o'the isle, sirrah?

STEPHANO I should have been a sore one then.

ALONSO This is a strange thing as e'er I looked on.   *Points to Caliban*

PROSPERO He is as disproportioned in his manners
As in his shape. Go, sirrah, to my cell:
330   Take with you your companions: as you look
To have my pardon, trim it handsomely.

CALIBAN Ay, that I will: and I'll be wise hereafter,
And seek for grace. What a thrice-double ass
Was I to take this drunkard for a god
335   And worship this dull fool!

PROSPERO Go to, away!

ALONSO Hence, and bestow your luggage where you
found it.

SEBASTIAN Or stole it, rather.

              [Exeunt Caliban, Stephano and Trinculo]

---

307 deal ... power could adopt some of the moon's power without its authority/could operate beyond the reach of the moon's power **309 bastard** illegitimate/hybrid **316 reeling ripe** drunk and staggering **317 gilded** flushed/enlivened **318 pickle** trouble/inebriation/state of being preserved in liquor **320 will ... bones** (the alcohol) will never leave my body **321 fly-blowing** decay (the blow-fly lays eggs in dead flesh) **324 cramp** i.e. doubled-up from either the pinches of Ariel's torment or drunkenness **325 sirrah** sir (contemptuous) **326 sore** aching/dreadful **328 manners** behaviour/moral conduct **331 trim it handsomely** adorn the cell beautifully **333 grace** mercy, direction **thrice-double** sixfold (three times two)

340 PROSPERO Sir, I invite your highness and your train
        To my poor cell, where you shall take your rest
        For this one night: which, part of it, I'll waste
        With such discourse as I not doubt shall make it
        Go quick away: the story of my life
345   And the particular accidents gone by
        Since I came to this isle: and in the morn
        I'll bring you to your ship, and so to Naples,
        Where I have hope to see the nuptial
        Of these our dear-belovèd solemnized,
350   And thence retire me to my Milan, where
        Every third thought shall be my grave.
     ALONSO I long
        To hear the story of your life, which must
        Take the ear strangely.
355 PROSPERO I'll deliver all,
        And promise you calm seas, auspicious gales
        And sail so expeditious that shall catch
        Your royal fleet far off.— My Ariel, chick,
        That is thy charge: then to the elements
360   Be free, and fare thou well.— Please you, draw near.
                            Exeunt [all but Prospero]
     EPILOGUE SPOKEN BY PROSPERO
        Now my charms are all o'erthrown,
        And what strength I have's mine own,
        Which is most faint: now 'tis true,
        I must be here confined by you,
365   Or sent to Naples. Let me not,
        Since I have my dukedom got
        And pardoned the deceiver, dwell
        In this bare island by your spell,
        But release me from my bands
370   With the help of your good hands:
        Gentle breath of yours my sails
        Must fill, or else my project fails,
        Which was to please. Now I want
        Spirits to enforce, art to enchant,

---

342 **waste** pass away   345 **accidents** events   349 **solemnized** marked with ceremony   351 **Every ...
grave** i.e. I will frequently meditate on death, as a good Christian should   354 **Take ... strangely** be an
extraordinary, captivating thing to hear   357 **expeditious** swift   **catch** catch up with   360 **draw near**
probably an invitation to the others to approach his cell, but the phrase also means 'attend', thus preparing
the audience for the epilogue   362 **charms ... o'erthrown** magic is relinquished (**o'erthrown** plays on the
sense of 'usurped')   364 **you** the audience   369 **bands** bonds   370 **hands** i.e. in applause   371 **Gentle
breath** kind words/cries of approval   373 **want** lack

375 And my ending is despair,
    Unless I be relieved by prayer,
    Which pierces so, that it assaults
    Mercy itself, and frees all faults.
        As you from crimes would pardoned be,
380   Let your indulgence set me free.   *Awaits applause*
                                                        Exit

---

376 **prayer** approbation and forgiveness   377 **pierces** ... **assaults** penetrates so deeply that it moves
380 **indulgence** approval (playing on the Catholic sense of 'official release from sin')

TEXTUAL NOTES

F = First Folio text of 1623, the only authority for the play
F2 = a correction introduced in the Second Folio text of 1632
Ed = a correction introduced by a later editor
SD = stage direction
SH = speech heading (i.e. speaker's name)

List of parts *based on 'Names of the Actors' (reordered) at end of* F *text*

1.1.8 SD *Ferdinand* = Ed. F = *Ferdinando* **65 wi'th'** = Ed. F = with'
1.2.129 wi'th' = Ed. F = with **202 princes** = Ed. F = Princesse *(old spelling of 'princes')* **330 she** = Ed. F = he
2.2.180 trencher = Ed. F = *trenchering*
3.1.2 sets = Ed. F = set **15 least** = F2. F = lest
3.2.127 scout = Ed. F = *cout (***128** F = *skowt)*
3.3.2 ache = F2. F = akes **34 islanders** = F2. F = Islands
4.1.12 gainst = Ed. F = Against *(beginning new half-line)* **13 guest** = F. *Some eds emend to* gift. **57 abstemious** = F2. F = abstenious **67 vetches** *spelled* Fetches *in* F **80 Her** = Ed. F = here **119 SH CERES** = Ed. *(no change of singer in* F *)* **134 wise** = F. *Some eds emend to* wife **209 them on** = Ed. F = on them
5.1.18 run = F2. F = runs **77 Didst** = F *(catchword on sig. B2v; text reads* Did*)* **87 lies** = Ed. F = ly **118 Whether** = Ed. F = Where **292 *Coraggio . . . coraggio*** = F2. F = *Coragio . . . Corasio*

SCENE-BY-SCENE ANALYSIS

ACT 1 SCENE 1

The play opens dramatically on board a ship in the middle of a violent storm. It features two sets of characters: mariners and nobles. Social hierarchy is overturned as the sailors give the orders, telling the aristocrats to keep out of the way. Despite their best efforts though, by the end of the scene, all agree that they and the ship are lost. The scene is characterized by the peril of the situation and the vitality of the Boatswain's language. It opens the debate on issues of sovereignty, authority and legitimacy, character, fate and predestination.

ACT 1 SCENE 2

A long scene which introduces the inhabitants of the island and the relationships between them. It raises questions of personal claims to authority and sovereignty over the island as divergent accounts of individual histories are related.

Lines 1–218: Reveals that the storm was not a product of nature but conjured up by Prospero. His daughter, Miranda, is distressed by the suffering of the victims but he reassures her that all are safe. Laying his magic cloak aside, he explains his real identity and how they came to the island. He is the rightful Duke of Milan and relates how twelve years ago with the support of the King of Naples, his brother Antonio usurped his dukedom. He and Miranda were set adrift in a small boat but survived thanks to one of the courtiers, Gonzalo, who took pity on them and furnished them with necessities for the voyage as well as Prospero's books. He speaks with bitterness of his brother Antonio's treachery, but by his own account, his neglect of civic duty in favour of private study played a role in encouraging his ambition. He goes on to explain his reason for raising this storm: his enemies were all on board ship: Fortune has delivered them into his hands. To what extent is a providential, benign destiny at work in shaping the course of events?

Lines 219–357: While Miranda sleeps, Ariel appears to do his master's bidding. He describes how he performed and managed the tempest and has since dispersed the shipwrecked passengers around the island. Prospero has further tasks for him but Ariel reminds his master of his promise to restore his liberty. Prospero is enraged, reminding Ariel in turn of the debt of gratitude he owes. When he and Miranda arrived, the island was not deserted. Ariel had originally been servant to the witch Sycorax, herself banished to the island while pregnant with her son, Caliban. Because he refused to carry out her wicked commands, Sycorax had imprisoned Ariel for twelve years in a cloven pine, during which time she died. He suffered great pains until Prospero finally released him. Prospero threatens that he will imprison Ariel in an oak if he refuses to obey him, though he promises to discharge him in two days' time. Ariel is now to turn himself into an invisible sea-nymph.

Lines 358–437: As Ariel departs, Prospero wakes Miranda, suggesting that they visit Caliban, now their slave. Miranda confesses her dislike of him but Prospero reminds her that they need him to perform all the menial tasks essential to their comfort and survival. The relationship between Prospero and Caliban is hostile and full of recriminations. Caliban curses him and Prospero responds with threats. Caliban relates his own version of Prospero's arrival on the island. Initially a mutually beneficial relationship, Prospero taught him to speak his language and he willingly showed them 'all the qualities o'th'isle'. He resents Prospero's assumption of kingship: 'For I am all the subjects that you have, / Which first was mine own king'. Prospero, however, disputes this account and accuses Caliban of having tried to violate Miranda sexually.

Whatever he says, though, Caliban dare not disobey Prospero's powerful magic.

Lines 438–590: The now invisible Ariel returns singing and playing music. Ferdinand, shipwrecked son of the King of Naples, follows the sounds. Miranda and Ferdinand meet. Each initially thinks the other a divinity from another world. Prospero accuses Ferdinand of being a traitor. Miranda defends him but Prospero remains impervious. Secretly, however, he's delighted that the young people are falling in love and praises Ariel's work. Miranda comforts Ferdinand.

Responses to Prospero and Caliban are crucial in determining overall interpretation of the play: Prospero's language and threats betray his unquestioning assumption of authority as well as his irascible temper; Caliban's stubborn defiance, his sense of injustice and ill-usage. The island is a microcosm which tests its inhabitants socially and morally, posing the issue of nature or nurture as the determinant factor in individual constitution, but this is not an isolated social laboratory; on the contrary, the shadows of the past haunt all the characters who have to resolve ancient inherited contentions.

ACT 2 SCENE 1

The rest of the aristocratic survivors of the storm are together, attempting to come to terms with their situation. The attitude of each to their misadventure defines their character.

Lines 1–151: The elderly courtier, Gonzalo, and the younger Adrian and Francisco are determined to be positive while Antonio and Sebastian jeer at them from the sidelines. Alonso is griefstricken by the loss, as he believes, of his son, Ferdinand. His brother, Sebastian, however, blames Alonso himself for the disaster by his determination to marry his daughter, Claribel, to the King of Tunis, an African on the far side of the Mediterranean. They were on the return voyage home when the tempest struck. The discussion of the wedding relates to another issue which the play raises: patriarchal control of daughters and the function of marriage in securing dynastic inheritance, a relevant theme in relation to Ferdinand and Miranda.

Lines 152–195: Gonzalo offers his own idealized prescription for sovereignty as he imagines himself as king of the island.

Lines 196–367: Ariel, still invisible, puts everyone to sleep except Antonio and Sebastian. Antonio proposes that they kill Alonso so that Sebastian can become King of Naples. His speech reveals a complete moral bankruptcy as he dismisses Sebastian's objections on the grounds of conscience. They are about to put their plan into action when Ariel intervenes once more to wake the other courtiers.

ACT 2 SCENE 2

Caliban enters carrying wood, still cursing Prospero and complaining of his ill-treatment. When he sees Trinculo he believes him to be a spirit sent to torment him and hides himself on the ground. Unable to identify this curious creature, Trinculo nevertheless immediately recognizes his potential for exploitation. If he were in England people would pay good money to see this 'strange fish' (l. 27). Trinculo fears another storm and takes shelter with the creature as the storm breaks. The drunken Stephano arrives but Caliban mistakes his tuneless singing for another punishment and begs him to stop. Stephano is bemused by the appearance of the 'monster' and he too thinks of taking him back to Naples as a prize for his own profit. He offers Caliban a drink, but, recognizing his friend's voice, Trinculo greets the butler. Stephano is by now thoroughly confused by the two-headed, four-legged monster. He finally disengages Trinculo and the two celebrate their reunion. Caliban, meanwhile, takes him for a god and his liquor for celestial drink. He agrees to serve him and in a reprise of Prospero's arrival immediately offers to show them around the island. Believing that the royal party are all drowned, Stephano suggests that he and Trinculo can now inherit the island. Meanwhile, Caliban is delighted to have exchanged masters and leads them off singing drunkenly.

The attitudes of the two strangers to the island towards its native inhabitants are callous, opportunistic and self-serving. Caliban, meanwhile, is revealed to be ingenuous and naive.

ACT 3 SCENE 1

Ferdinand enters carrying wood, but, in contrast to Caliban, is happy to perform this menial task because of his love for Miranda, despite her father's harshness towards him. She visits him and offers to carry the logs herself. He refuses and asks her name, which, against her father's injunction, she tells him. Ferdinand then confesses his deep admiration and love and she innocently acknowledges her own. Unbeknownst to them both, Prospero has been watching the scene.

ACT 3 SCENE 2

Caliban, Stephano and Trinculo are drunk. Caliban and Trinculo quarrel. Stephano, however, defends Caliban and threatens to hang Trinculo. Caliban then relates his own history and tells them about Prospero and Miranda. He details plans for Prospero's murder, dwelling on the need to destroy his books (ll. 95–97). The interventions of the invisible Ariel lead to further contention. Again Stephano restores peace and they set off to kill Prospero and make Stephano king of the island and Miranda his queen. The sound of Ariel's music instils fear in the others, but in a passage of arresting poetry Caliban reassures them about the island and its 'noises, / Sounds and sweet airs' (ll. 141–149). They follow the music offstage.

ACT 3 SCENE 3

The courtiers are tired and weary of wandering round the island seeking Ferdinand. They rest while Antonio and Sebastian in asides reiterate their plan to murder Alonso at the next opportunity.

Meanwhile Prospero, now invisible, enters accompanied by the sounds of music and by 'strange shapes' who set out a banquet. The courtiers are amazed but prepare to eat when they are interrupted by thunder and lightning. Ariel enters as a harpy this time and causes the banquet to vanish. He addresses Alonso, Sebastian and Antonio as 'three men of sin' (l. 64). As they draw their swords he tells them that he and his fellows are invulnerable and goes on to relate his real concern, their part in Prospero's overthrow many years before, for which reason they are now being punished and Alonso is 'bereft' of his son (l. 87). Ariel vanishes in another clap of thunder and the shapes re-enter to remove the table. Prospero congratulates Ariel on his performance and the fact that his enemies are now in his power. Alonso is deeply affected by the experience, wishing only to join his son (ll. 107–114). Gonzalo fears that the 'great guilt' of the three will make them desperate.

ACT 4 SCENE 1

The fourth act comprises one long running scene.

Lines 1–65: Prospero explains to Ferdinand that his harsh treatment was designed as a test of his character and love. Having passed the test he is rewarded by being given Miranda in marriage, with the warning that any premarital sex would curse their union. Ferdinand reassures him that his thoughts are chaste. Prospero tells them to sit and calls for Ariel, who is now to bring 'the rabble' to that place. In the meantime Prospero plans a demonstration of his magical arts for the pair.

Lines 66–177: He stages a nuptial masque of the goddesses Iris, Juno and Ceres to celebrate 'A contract of true love'. Ferdinand is impressed by the spectacle: the goddesses are then joined by a group of pastoral rustics and they dance gracefully together until Prospero suddenly remembers Caliban's plot to kill him. The masque figures vanish instantly. Prospero attempts to disguise his fury before Ferdinand and Miranda in a speech which has been regarded by some critics as a rehearsal of Shakespeare's own symbolic farewell to the theatre, 'Our revels now are ended. These our actors, / As I foretold you, were all spirits and / Are melted into air, into thin air' (ll. 161–171). He tells Ferdinand and Miranda to retire to his cell.

Lines 178–270: Ariel describes how he has led Caliban and his companions into a foul pool. Prospero praises him and orders him to fetch fine clothing. Meanwhile, Prospero complains of Caliban's inherent wickedness and threatens further punishment. Ariel returns with the clothes. Caliban warns Stephano and Trinculo to be wary but they are disgruntled by their recent drubbing. As soon as they see the finery, they want to put it on, despite Caliban's efforts to concentrate their minds on murder. He is disgusted by their frivolity but Stephano threatens banishment from the island, which he regards as his kingdom, if Caliban refuses to carry the clothes back to his wine store.

Lines 271–283: A noise is heard and spirits enter as dogs and hounds who chase the three, while Prospero threatens further punishments. Now all his enemies are at his mercy and his labours nearly ended. Ariel is promised his freedom very soon.

ACT 5 SCENE 1

Again, one long scene in which all the characters finally assemble and many of the confusions and issues are resolved.

Lines 1–37: Prospero sees his project 'gather to a head'. Ariel tells him that Alonso, Alonso's brother Sebastian, and Prospero's brother Antonio, are all prisoners, paralysed by enchantment until he releases them. The others, meanwhile, weep over their fate. Ariel, though, tells Prospero that he believes if he were to see them for himself, he too would feel pity for them, as he would himself if he were human. Prospero is struck by the irony of the non-human Ariel feeling human sympathy for these creatures. The lesson in humanity chastens him and he vows that he will indeed take pity on them. He tells Ariel to release them and he will restore them to their senses.

Lines 38–108: As Ariel departs Prospero conjures for the last time, resolving to give up all his charms and spells: 'But this rough magic / I here abjure' (ll. 55–56), to break his staff and drown his book. Ariel returns with the courtiers who enter Prospero's magic circle. He addresses each in turn: quieting Alonso's distress, blessing Gonzalo's kindness, and even forgiving his brother, Antonio. They don't recognize him dressed as he is, so he sends Ariel for his hat and rapier, and then sends him to rouse the mariners, safe asleep on the ship.

Lines 109–245: Prospero, now in his courtly garments, turns to the nobles again and tells them who he is. Alonso, at first incredulous, begs forgiveness for past wrongdoing. Prospero embraces Gonzalo and forgives Antonio, who, on a disturbing note in the general atmosphere of harmony and reconciliation, fails to respond. Alonso asks for particulars of his story and how he arrived on this shore where he fears his son has been lost. Prospero explains that he too has lost a daughter which leads Alonso to exclaim that he wishes they were both alive and King and Queen of Naples. Prospero says that his story will have to be told another day, but leads Alonso to his cell where he reveals Ferdinand and Miranda together playing chess. Miranda accuses Ferdinand of cheating. He exclaims that he would not do such a thing, but with a surprising touch of realpolitik, Miranda suggests that 'for a score of kingdoms you should wrangle, / And I would call it fair play' (ll. 192–193). Alonso and Ferdinand are reunited, even Sebastian is touched and Miranda amazed by the sight of so many new faces: 'O brave new world, / That has such people in't' (ll. 205–206). Ferdinand tells his father that Miranda is to be his wife. Alonso is immediately reconciled and questions whether the events might not record the workings of a providential design: 'Was Milan thrust from Milan that his issue / Should become kings of Naples?' (ll. 233–234).

Lines 246–289: Ariel appears followed by the ship's Master and Boatswain; the latter announces that all are safe and the ship is ready to sail. Alonso is convinced that all these events are unnatural. Prospero endeavours to set his mind at rest. He praises Ariel and asks him finally to bring Caliban, Stephano and Trinculo to him.

Lines 290–339: They appear still in their finery. Caliban recognizes that Prospero too is in his finery and fears that he will be punished. Prospero identifies Caliban to the other nobles and tells them about the plot to murder him. They must know who the other two are, but Caliban he finally acknowledges as belonging to him, 'this thing of darkness I / Acknowledge mine' (ll. 311–312). He tells Caliban to go to his cell with his companions and prepare it for the company. Caliban now realizes his folly in worshipping the pair and promises to 'seek for grace' (l. 333) in future.

Lines 340–360: Prospero invites the whole company to his cell to rest for one night during which he will relate the events of his life and how he came to the island. He will then accompany them all to Naples for the marriage of Ferdinand and Miranda. Afterwards he will retire to Milan to contemplate old age and death. He promises them a good voyage and finally releases Ariel.

As the other characters leave the stage, Prospero delivers the Epilogue in which he tells the audience that he has no more magic, only his own strength. He must therefore be confined to the island unless they release him by the power of their breath and hands, and begs indulgence for his sins as the audience too would wish to be pardoned. This meta-theatrical conclusion seems to round off the play on a positive note, but a brief reflection reveals that the most complex problems have been left unresolved and the future for many of the characters is far from clear. The departing spectator is left wondering if Antonio is really reconciled to his brother's return, exactly what Prospero means when he has said that 'every third thought' will be his 'grave', where Ariel will go now that he is free, and what will happen to Caliban – is he to remain on the island, its lonely king once more, or will he accompany Prospero to Milan?

THE TEMPEST IN PERFORMANCE: THE RSC AND BEYOND

The best way to understand a Shakespeare play is to see it or ideally to participate in it. By examining a range of productions, we may gain a sense of the extraordinary variety of approaches and interpretations that are possible – a variety that gives Shakespeare his unique capacity to be reinvented and made 'our contemporary' four centuries after his death.

We begin with a brief overview of the play's theatrical and cinematic life, offering historical perspectives on how it has been performed. We then analyse in more detail a series of productions staged over the last half-century by the Royal Shakespeare Company. The sense of dialogue between productions that can only occur when a company is dedicated to the revival and investigation of the Shakespeare canon over a long period, together with the uniquely comprehensive archival resource of promptbooks, programme notes, reviews and interviews held on behalf of the RSC at the Shakespeare Birthplace Trust in Stratford-upon-Avon, allows an 'RSC stage history' to become a crucible in which the chemistry of the play can be explored.

Finally, we go to the horse's mouth. Modern theatre is dominated by the figure of the director. He, or sometimes she (like musical conducting, theatre directing remains a male-dominated profession), must hold together the whole play, whereas the actor must concentrate on his or her part. The director's viewpoint is therefore especially valuable. Shakespeare's plasticity is wonderfully revealed when we hear directors of highly successful productions answering the same questions in very different ways.

FOUR CENTURIES OF *THE TEMPEST*: AN OVERVIEW

The Tempest's first recorded performance was at the court of James I on Hallowmass Night, 1 November 1611.[1] In 1613 it was performed at court again, this time as one of fourteen plays chosen to celebrate the marriage of James I's daughter Elizabeth to the Elector Palatine.[2] These performances and the masque in Act 4 have sometimes suggested a special association with the Jacobean court. However, the effects called for in the masque – descents, ascents and the use of a trapdoor – all suggest performance in the public theatres used by the King's Men, the Globe and the smaller indoor Blackfriars Theatre.

This was one of the first of Shakespeare's plays to be revived after the Restoration and the reopening of the theatres. Samuel Pepys saw the first performance in 1667:

> at noon resolve with Sir W. Penn to go see *The Tempest*, an old play of Shakespeare's acted here the first day ... the most innocent play that ever I saw .... The play is no great wit; but yet good, above ordinary plays.[3]

The 'old play of Shakespeare's' described by Pepys was not, however, Shakespeare's *Tempest* but an adaptation by Sir William Davenant and John Dryden called *The Tempest, or The Enchanted Island* which developed the plot to suit Restoration tastes and capitalized on the newly permitted presence of women onstage by inventing a sister for Miranda called Dorinda, together with the cross-dressed 'breeches' part of Hippolito, Prospero's ward. Sycorax became Caliban's sister and even Ariel had a female consort, Milcha. Whereas scholars were busy recovering Shakespeare's text for published editions from the early eighteenth century, this adaptation, and a revised operatic version by Thomas Shadwell with music by Henry Purcell dating from 1674, supplanted Shakespeare's on the stage for more than a century and a half. They had machinery, elaborate effects, spectacular staging and music, and proved immensely profitable and popular with London theatre-goers. The highlight seems to have been the storm scene which was moved to Act 2 in order to accommodate latecomers. This adaptation in turn spawned Thomas Duffett's obscene burlesque, *The Mock Tempest, or the Enchanted Castle*, in which Miranda and Dorinda feature as prostitutes.

David Garrick had briefly presented Shakespeare's original play, with some cuts in the mid-eighteenth century, but in the next generation John Philip Kemble returned to the Restoration version. When Shakespeare's text was finally restored by William Charles Macready in 1838, the spectacular staging of the storm scene and the masque were fixed theatrical traditions which Macready retained, together with much of the music. By the end of the nineteenth century two contrasting production modes were evident – the elaborate spectacle, exemplified by directors such as Herbert Beerbohm Tree in London and Augustin Daly in New York, which offered scenic staging and pantomimic action with a full orchestral score versus the innovatory pared-down productions by F. R. Benson at Stratford and William Poel's Elizabethan Stage Society which used a bare set on an open stage.

The dominant theme in twentieth-century productions was the exploration of the play as colonial experience, evident even in the pro-imperial Beerbohm Tree production of 1904. Romanticism had changed attitudes to Caliban and it was Macready's 1838 revival of Shakespeare's text that 'confirmed ... the romantic critics' more sympathetic conceptions of Caliban'.[4] As Vaughan and Vaughan record, it was in this production that 'the modern Caliban, victim of oppression, was born'.[5] Caliban became less comic but more monstrous; when in 1854 in New York the leading comic actor William Burton took the part in his own theatre, the anonymous *New York Times* reviewer records how

A wild creature on all fours sprang upon the stage, with claws on his hands, and some weird animal arrangement about the head partly like a snail. It was an immense conception. Not the great God Pan himself was more the link between the man and the beast than this thing. It was a creature of the woods, one of nature's spawns; it breathed of nuts and herbs, and rubbed itself against the back of trees.[6]

Charles Kean's 1857 Caliban had similarly animal overtones suggesting 'the dawn of the apish Caliban'[7] which dominated stage versions towards the end of the nineteenth century, influenced by Daniel Wilson's *Caliban, the Missing Link* (1873) in which Shakespeare's creation of the misshapen Caliban suggested the Bard's intuitive grasp of evolutionary theory.

Actor-managers Beerbohm Tree and F. R. Benson both chose to play Caliban in preference to Prospero. Benson's wife records how her husband 'spent many hours watching monkeys and baboons in the Zoo, in order to get the movements and postures in keeping with his "make-up"', in a costume which she described as 'half-monkey, half coco-nut', noting that he 'delighted in swarming up a tree on the stage and hanging from the branches head downwards while he gibbered at "Trinculo"'.[8] Tyrone Power in Daly's 1897 production invoked the same idea. According to William Winter, the *New York Daily Tribune* reviewer, he played Caliban as a 'brutish creature, the hideous, malignant clod of evil, in whom, nevertheless, the germs of intelligence, feeling and fanciful perception are beginning to stir'.[9] Beerbohm Tree's Caliban in 1904 stressed Caliban's humanity, arguing that 'in his love of music and his affinity with the unseen world, we discern in the soul which inhabits the brutish body of this elemental man the germs of a sense of beauty, the dawn of art'.[10] The production's most famous scene was the final tableau showing Caliban alone once more on his island as the Neapolitans sailed for home:

Caliban *creeps from his cave and watches* .... Caliban *listens for the last time to the sweet air* [Ariel's song], *then turns sadly in the direction of the departing ship. The play is ended. As the curtain rises again, the ship is seen on the horizon,* Caliban *stretching out his arms toward it in mute despair. The night falls, and* Caliban *is left on the lonely rock. He is king once more.*[11]

In the second half of the twentieth century Caliban has frequently been represented as black, initially by white actors in blackface. The first black actor to play the part was Canada Lee in Margaret Webster's 1945 New York production, although in many

1. Frank Benson as a fish-eating Caliban in the 1890s, represented as a creature akin to Charles Darwin's 'missing link' between ape and human.

ways his performance harked back to the monstrous representations of earlier productions: 'Lee wore a scaly costume and grotesque mask, moved with an animal-like crouch, and emphasized Caliban's monstrousness.'[12] In the past fifty years Caliban has evolved from comic grotesque to 'noble savage'. Jeanne Addison Roberts described Henry Baker's performance at the 1970 Washington Summer Festival Shakespeare production: 'Baker's black skin, his somewhat flawed enunciation, a minstrel-show mouth painted grotesquely in a greenish face, and the use of the word "slave" evoked instantly for the Washington audience the American Negro.'[13]

Baker's Caliban refused to be cowed or subdued: 'Caliban was now a black militant, angry and recalcitrant.'[14] In the same year Jonathan Miller's production at the Mermaid Theatre drew on Octave Mannoni's anthropological study of colonial oppression,

Prospero and Caliban,[15] which used these two characters as emblems of the colonial paradigm. One reviewer described Rudolph Walker's Caliban as 'an uneducated field Negro' in contrast to Norman Beaton's Ariel, a 'competent, educated "houseboy"'.[16] Historians of the play's afterlife regard the early 1980s as representing the 'climax of Caliban's politicization'[17] in productions around the world. It is perhaps as a reaction against this trend that directors in the early twenty-first century seem to have become interested in Ariel again.

Whereas Prospero had traditionally been regarded as an elderly benign father-figure, a tradition which continued well into the twentieth century, more recent productions have often cast a much younger man and explored the contradictions within the text to reveal a complex, demanding character. The actor most deeply associated with the role in the twentieth century was Sir John Gielgud who performed it four times in the theatre, the first time at the Old Vic in 1930 at the astonishingly young age of twenty-six. His interpretation evolved over the years and subsequent productions, culminating in the grave, beautiful performance in Peter Greenaway's extraordinary film adaptation, *Prospero's Books*. As one critic puts it,

> Gielgud has made the part very much his own, developing and deepening his interpretation over the years. From the rather nebulous shape of his first benevolent Prospero he has gradually explored the tensions and misgivings in the character so as to make him an altogether more dramatically complex and interesting figure. Through his successive assumptions of the part he has been instrumental in bringing about a revaluation of the play: a consideration of its serious themes as against an attitude to the work as an escapist romance dressed up in exotic trimmings and offering an opportunity for spectacular theatrical pyrotechnics.[18]

With the impact of 'realistic' media such as film and television, there has been renewed interest and focus on the theatricality of theatre and the meta-theatricality of *The Tempest* has been explored by a number of directors. In 1968 Peter Brook directed a radical

2. The play as magical spectacle, with elaborate design and Ariel centre-stage as harpy above the 'three men of sin': Shakespeare Memorial Theatre, Stratford-upon-Avon, 1951, directed by Michael Benthall and designed by Loudon Sainthill.

experimental production at the Roundhouse against a background of the cultural revolution of the 1960s which

> brought together players from France, Britain, Japan and the United States to explore theatrical techniques of expression. For the opening storm, for instance, a Japanese actor crouched vocalising sounds of wind and terror whilst the rest huddled together whimpering and trembling. It was an investigation of certain themes of the play, essentially mounted as an exercise for actors. It was, however, to bear fruit in many of Brook's subsequent productions, most notably his celebrated *Midsummer Night's Dream* in 1970.[19]

Peter Hall at the National Theatre in 1974 saw the play 'in terms of the Jacobean court masque and his staging was dominated by equivalents of the theatrical techniques which Inigo Jones introduced into England'.[20] Prospero took on the role of stage manager. Four years later Giorgio Strehler directed a spectacular Italian version with the Piccolo Teatro of Milan, Italy's most celebrated and long-established repertory company. His production lasted for four hours and was widely acclaimed for its 'overwhelming theatrical force and seriousness of purpose'.[21] The central focus was on Prospero and Ariel, converting 'their relationship into a metaphor for the interaction of director and actor' with spectacle the keynote:

> Strehler's production opened with a spectacular storm lasting fifteen minutes. Behind a huge transparent canvas an open-sailed ship was visible. Sailors clambered up the ropes; the rigging collapsed; the mast split. Throughout this scene vast blue waves billowed and rolled round the stage, created by huge lengths of blue silk – five thousand square yards of it – operated by sixteen unseen operators hidden under the stage, which was divided into three corridors with their floor shaped into mounds and hollows. Musicians beat drums, stage hands operated thunder sheets, and technicians provided bursts of lightning. It was in two senses a 'direful *spectacle*': terrifying but at the same time clearly the product of theatrical artifice. Finally the waves retreated as the strips of silk were drawn back to reveal a simple wooden raft which represented the island.[22]

George C. Wolfe's 1994–95 New York Shakespeare Festival production likewise employed spectacular staging effects, described here by Robert Brustein:

> Bunraku puppets, Indonesian shadow play, Caribbean carnivals, Macy's Day floats, Asian stilt-walkers, death masks, stick dancing, magical transformations effected through a haze of smokepots. Don't look to spend any quiet time here. The stage is in constant motion. This may be the busiest *Tempest* in history.[23]

If Prospero was traditionally seen as a benign omniscient father-figure, Miranda had been regarded as the perfect daughter. In the light of feminist thinking, Prospero's treatment of his daughter and his plans for her future have been seen as an unwholesome desire for patriarchal control. Miranda's problematic position in colonial discourse has been discussed to the point that Shakespeare scholar Ann Thompson has posed the question, 'What kind of pleasure can a woman and a feminist take in this text beyond the rather grim one of mapping its various patterns of exploitation?'[24] The relationship between father and daughter has accordingly undergone a variety of representations and the lines restored which previous ages thought impossible for Miranda to utter, 'Abhorrèd slave, / Which any print of goodness wilt not take, / Being capable of all ill' (1.2.411–413).

Productions of *The Tempest* in the late twentieth and early twenty-first centuries have explored many possibilities, adapting it to a variety of styles, ideological inflexions and locales, playing on its supreme flexibility; Jonathan Kent's 2001 watery Almeida Theatre production was set on an island littoral and in the same year the role of Prospero was played by a woman, Vanessa Redgrave, at the reconstructed Shakespeare's Globe.

The Tempest has been all things to all those concerned with the nature of theatre. It has also proved an inspiration in the cinema, from a brief early silent version of 1908 to the 1956 sci-fi adaptation directed by Fred Wilcox, *The Forbidden Planet* (itself the inspiration for the 1989 camp sci-fi rock and roll musical, *Return to the Forbidden Planet*) to Derek Jarman's (1979) film *The Tempest*, a compelling, dreamlike personal vision, shot in the decaying gothic mansion Stoneleigh Abbey, to Paul Mazursky's 1982 banal urban update (*Tempest*), and finally Peter Greenaway's visually spectacular re-imagining of the play to produce a meditation on the power of art culminating in book number 24, a folio volume of 1623, consisting of thirty-six plays, *Prospero's Books*.

AT THE RSC

> *The Tempest* ... distils the poetic essence of the whole Shakespearean universe.
>> (Programme notes to 1963 RSC production, quoting G. Wilson Knight, 1932)

Freedom and oppression, obedience and rebellion, and the corruption of power in both personal and political life are housed in this most mysterious of Shakespeare's 'comedies'. Ideas of kingship, fatherhood, authority and love inform the three divergent plot lines, coming together in a final scene of revelation and reconciliation.

The Tempest offers us a world in which its characters operate free from society's constraints – but what type of world is it, and what is the nature of the characters that inhabit it? As Anne Barton pointed out in the programme notes to John Barton's 1970 Royal Shakespeare Company production, 'To perform it in the theatre, even to try and talk about it, is inevitably to add to its substance by filling in gaps and silences left deliberately by the dramatist.' Peter Brook, who directed the play for the Shakespeare Memorial Theatre in Stratford-upon-Avon in 1957, and co-directed it in 1963 for the RSC with Clifford Williams, discussed the difficult nature of coming to grips with Shakespeare's most elusive of plays:

> When we see how nothing in the play is what it seems, how it takes place on an island and not on an island, during a day and not during a day, with a tempest that sets off a series of events that are still within a tempest even when the storm is done, that the charming pastoral for children naturally encompasses rape, murder, conspiracy and violence; when we begin to unearth the themes that Shakespeare so carefully buried, we see that it is his final statement, and that it deals with the whole condition of man.[25]

A play of infinite possibilities, notoriously difficult to stage effectively, *The Tempest* offers a multitude of choices for its director and a conundrum for actors seeking to build dimension from

Shakespeare's enigmatic characterizations. Shakespeare scholar Christine Dymkowski outlines some of the play's dualities:

> It seems unusually elastic, its almost miraculous flexibility allowing it to embody radically different interpretations, characterisations and emphases. Prospero and Caliban can not only exchange places as hero and villain, but also vie with each other to occupy both places at once. Ariel can be female or male, a willing or an unwilling servant. Miranda can seem an innocent maiden, a hoydenish tomboy or a rebellious teenager. Antonio can seek forgiveness from his brother or remain sinister until the end. Stephano and Trinculo can present themselves as harmless buffoons or dangerous louts. The island can appear a lush paradise or a barren desert or both at once. The narrative can speak for or against racism or turn into a psychological thriller. The play's final effect can be one of decay and despair or renewal and hope.[26]

All interpreters of the play, whether directors in the rehearsal room or critics in the study, have to address difficult questions about the portrayal of Prospero, the nature of his 'rough magic' and how he interacts with the other characters, most importantly Ariel and Caliban.

Designing the Enchanted Isle

In the theatre or on screen, a key interpretive choice for director and designer is the representation of the setting in which the action takes place: the island that is the location for the entire action after the initial shipboard storm. The play is readily transportable to different settings and periods. The island's imprecise location makes it a place of the imagination; perhaps more than any other Shakespearean location, it is open to multitudinous interpretations. *The Tempest* has been set in all the continents of the world, and even in outer space.

Modern directors have moved away from the nineteenth-century taste for spectacular stage pictures, and considered alternative means of depicting the island's magical environment. So, for instance, Rupert Goold's 2006 RSC production achieved many notable effects, not least through its surprising setting:

> The shipwrecked nobles have washed up in the Arctic or some more metaphoric, spiritually desolate realm ... during the storm, grey waves crash on a huge projection scrim, a radar dial transforms into a porthole-cum-magic circle through which we spy below-decks, then a black screen whirls with white flecks as if charting a tornado or brainwave interference. It's a startling vision, as is the panorama of jagged ice that comprises Prospero's isle and evokes Caspar David Friedrich's bleak painting, *The Wreck of the Hope*.[27]

Just over forty years before, the designer for the RSC's 1963 production, Abd'Elkader Farrah, created an abstract world of 'strange suns and moons, space-creatures who act as Ariel's assistants; trapdoors by the dozen, ever-opening to emit some fresh wonder, or walls that fall, crashing, at a wave of Prospero's wand'.[28] He believed that elaborate settings were no longer appropriate in the cinematic age: 'I could have conjured up a romantic sea-storm: wind, rain, ship cracking, and so on. It would have made a big impact. But the cinema does such things better.'[29] The director of this production, Clifford Williams, also stated: 'The play is termed a romance, but you can't present a romance in romantic terms – the baroque, the rococo; we don't respond to them any more.'[30]

Although this 1963 production was referred to as gimmicky and failed to impress an unprepared theatrical world, it marked a sea change in the way directors thought about the play and how the RSC designed its productions. The company's next three productions also worked with pared-down abstract sets, and it was not until 1982, almost twenty years later, that a more elaborate design returned to the main stage at Stratford-upon-Avon. Abstract settings encouraged a more cerebral reading of the play, prompting us to think of the plays characters as being metaphorical, aspects of Prospero's mind, whereas designs which created a more formulated environment often threw the focus of the play on more external issues such as kingship, inheritance, revenge, treachery and colonialism.

The stage design alone can often indicate what type of interpretation we are about to experience. Directors today have the visual freedom of expression to conduct an examination of many of the things that the play makes us ponder: the corrupting influence of power and revenge, the complexity of Prospero's mind, or the use of the play as a means of looking at the very nature of theatre itself. The following three RSC productions (1982, 1988 and 1993) took on these different challenges in imaginative ways. The skeletal shape of the wreck of Prospero's ship dominated the set for the 1982 Ron Daniels production.

> In the opening storm scene, a boat's prow pushes out towards the audience while the beleaguered crew do valiant battle with the sound effects. A large black sail billows in the wind. Prospero's island is then revealed as a broken ship of state, with a severely crushed foredeck, leaning mast with crow's nest, and tattered sails .... This is a strong visual conception that underlines the political upheavals back home in Milan and establishes Prospero as an exiled magician rather than an eccentric conjurer. The masques and apparitions are produced from behind the ship's defunct main sail: Caliban enters from below deck through a trapdoor, and Ariel and this fellow sprites nip speedily about the boat like willing versatile cabin boys.[31]

Ned Chaillet of *The Times* described it as a production of

> All glitter and light, all colour and hooped skirts with collars of shining wire and air. The beastly terrors invoked and unleashed on the conspiracy of fools led by Caliban are misshapen demons with glowing eyes, preceded by the baying skeletons of dogs.[32]

The 'hyper realistic wreck'[33] of the ship housed the characters and confined the action of the play within its limits. This was Prospero's ship and his magic emanated from the core of a corrupted vessel. The nature of his magic was morally ambiguous, and the set indicated a corruption in both the man and the state of Milan, which he once represented. As Michael Billington said in his review, this production never let the spectator forget that 'this is a play about power' and about the 'internal struggle between Prospero's own omnipotence and humanity'.[34]

In order to emphasize a more cerebral reading of the play, the 1988 RSC production, directed by Nicholas Hytner, returned to the use of a pared-down set. A white, shaped disc on which the action took place successfully symbolized the magic island and Prospero's mind:

> On a disc of sun-whitened boards, framed by billows of shifting cloudscape, Nicholas Hytner's dream-Tempest unfolds. This circle, it seems, is Prospero's mind's eye ... the characters are the stuff of his dream, to be disposed of as he wishes.[35]

> The disc of an island (designed by David Fielding) is decorated with a single rock which looks disconcertingly like a jacket potato, but apart from this there is little to distract the eye. There is a marvellous sense that the island is decorated only by characters. Each seems a discovery washed up on shore, a curiosity to be inspected or a miracle to be wondered at.[36]

> The technical effects are sparingly and subtly used. The storm is evoked through strobe lighting. Ariel slithers up and down the sides of the proscenium arch and at one point descends in a flurry of angelic feathers. Prospero's acolytes are as shabbily dressed as their master. There is magic in the air but it is mainly achieved through Jeremy Sams's music and the rapid tonal shifts to arctic blue in Mark Henderson's lighting.[37]

These reviews would seem to suggest that this *Tempest*'s grip on the audience was achieved in no small measure by an *absence* of elaborate scenery, stage furniture and props. It encouraged the audience to view the stage, as the Elizabethans might have, as a blank space of the imagination on which Prospero can conjure his personal visions.

The design of Sam Mendes' 1993 production made a blatant statement about the meta-theatrical nature of the play. Benedict Nightingale of *The Times* pointed out that 'from the word go it is clear that the RSC's latest *Tempest* will not be tripping with sprites or bursting with pretty vegetation'.[38]

> The play began with a bare boarded stage, in the centre of which was a large property basket. An orange disk of sun lowered from a backdrop. As the house lights dimmed, a white-suited figure, Ariel, emerged deliberately from the basket, closed the lid, then stood on it and raised his hand to start the swing of a lantern lowered to him from the flies. Prospero was presently seen behind the gauze drop, watching from a ladder. There was no chance of a first-time spectator, unacquainted with the play, mistaking this action for anything but the representation of a fake storm. It established Ariel's power, a theme that ran through the production up to the climactic moment when, given his freedom by Prospero, he spat in the duke of Milan's face.[39]

Critic Michael Billington described how

> Mendes and the designer, Anthony Ward, present the play as a series of shifting illusions . . . . Other characters – such as Caliban and Trinculo, here played as a music-hall ventriloquist complete with recalcitrant doll – are taken out of the prop-basket as required. And Prospero himself is a Victorian dramatist-director writing his own script as he goes along: as he describes the Milanese usurpers to Miranda he conjures them up form behind a cloud-capped screen and when he stages the betrothal masque for the lovers he confronts them with a Pollocks Toy Theatre which is then magnified many times in reality. Illusion opens out within illusion as in a series of Chinese boxes.[40]

In portraying the set of *The Tempest* as a stage itself, an association was created in the audience's minds linking magician and playwright – Prospero as the auteur, the dramatist of his own world, creating characters and situations which often take on a life of their own and go beyond his control. This approach may give us a glimpse of Shakespeare's own thoughts about the creative process itself.

Playing Prospero

> The fascination of Prospero is that he's such an emotional jigsaw puzzle, loveable one minute, hateful the next, then vengeful, then sentimental. His moods change like quicksilver, which is very attractive to an actor.
>
> (Alec McCowen, actor)[41]

How to reconcile these varying moods and create a balanced performance that has narrative drive is the challenge presented to the actor. The 'refractory elements ... that have not yet found complete release'[42] – Prospero's feelings about his enemies, his hold on the island's magic – can drive the interpretation of the part in different directions: benign fatherly figure, authoritarian avenger, ruthless plotter, disenchanted melancholic. Whatever the choices made by the actor, his interpretation of Prospero will determine the outcome of the production.

> To focus on Prospero the magus, or to place the human duke at the centre – or to manage a reconciliation between the two – is one of the major decisions the actor must take. But whatever approach is adopted, the fact that Prospero controls virtually all the play's action means that it is only through and in him that real dramatic tension can be generated.[43]

In looking at two of the RSC's productions we can glean many of the perspectives and ideas that modern interpretations bring to the part. Michael Billington gives an indication of how Derek Jacobi (directed by Ron Daniels, 1982) and John Wood (directed by Nicholas Hytner, 1988) tackled the role:

> Instead of the usual benign headmaster dabbling in amateur magic, he offers a ferocious magus who has, in the Freudian manner, imposed his will on natural phenomena .... The tension comes from seeing how and when this Prospero will learn to love; and what is fascinating is that Mr Jacobi delays until the last second the access of charity ... only the sudden, silent appearance of Ariel at his side checks his ungovernable fury and leads to a hard-wrung, 'I do forgive thee'. Mr Jacobi brilliantly offers us a man who has elected to play God and who

finds it hard to return to the prosaic trappings of mortality ... its success lies in the way it shows Prospero using magic as an instrument of brute force and gradually shedding his divine arrogance.[44]

The tension and excitement in this production derive principally from John Wood's intellectually bracing Prospero. Biting irony, precise articulation and the suggestion of some internal demon are this actor's strong suits. The real key to the performance lies in its sense of tormented solitude .... Mr Wood presents us with an instinctive hermit in open-necked shirt and gardening trousers, who has sought refuge in magic and whose visible uneasiness with people shows itself when he is confronted by his enemies. It is a wholly persuasive reading: one that suggests Prospero is a Freudian wreck whose battles are all internal.[45]

We can see from these reviews that these actors have given two very different performances: Jacobi's full of 'angry drives and vengeful urges', which are 'eventually overcome by a willed adherence to human virtue';[46] Wood's 'wounded rather than an angry man',[47] introverted and distressed, his narrative 'a re-run of his agony, a condensation of long-endured grief'.[48]

Prospero's relationship to magic is central to these, and other, performances. When playing Prospero for the BBC, Michael Hordern questioned:

How are we to handle the magic in *The Tempest*? This is one of the great difficulties in presenting the play and in playing Prospero. A Jacobean audience would have been steeped in superstition, magic and the supernatural and so would have been in complete accord with Prospero's conjuring. Yet no amount of abracadabra, clever lighting effects and crystal balls in going to carry a modern audience to the suspension of disbelief.[49]

With magic no longer a reality to a modern audience, it has to be presented in a way that is believable for the audience. Costuming plays an important part in signifying the nature of the magician and his power. While conjuring, Jacobi's elaborate magical cloak took the form of a priestly vestment, with cabbalistic, astrological and alchemical symbols. The significance of this cloak was demonstrated by the fact that it filled a full page in the programme – the first image of Prospero seen before the performance began. The programme also contained extensive notes on 'ritual magic'. Prospero as all-powerful magus was clearly central to this production.

An inner emotional 'tempest' has brought a reality, a humanizing influence on recent performances. Jacobi's Prospero waged a continual psychological battle in which he consciously had to will himself back into a human frame of mind, as if dark forces temporarily possessed him. For Jacobi's Prospero the removal of the cloak physically dramatized an end to magical influence. His humanity was visually signified by a tattered costume – an old, worn dressing gown, ordinary shirt and trousers. Markedly younger than previous Prosperos, Jacobi commented:

> I am sure he is not old in body. I think he has grown old in his mind. His researchings into magic and his workings with the elements have made his brain old ... it has almost burned him out.[50]

Conversely, when in the grips of a spell he became revitalized. In his performance there was an obvious element of addiction to power, and a sexual potency in the power of magic that took a monumental effort for him relinquish.

The trend of having younger actors portray the role carried on into the next RSC production in 1988. Although of an age with Jacobi, John Wood's Prospero was physically very different. He was costumed in a modern 'open-necked shirt and baggy, unpressed flannels'.[51] A long, plain dressing gown served as his magic cloak, and a tall, thin wooden stick, which was often planted upright in the centre of the stage, served as his staff. Unlike Jacobi, he had none of the elaborate traditional trappings of the magus. The basic nature of his costume indicated his vulnerability to external influences, both supernatural and human.

3. Derek Jacobi as a Prospero in stern control of Miranda's betrothal to Ferdinand, with Michael Maloney and Alice Krige as the lovers, in Ron Daniels' 1982 RSC production.

Wood's mode of verse speaking indicated that the uncanny, otherworldly influence of magical chants and Ariel's songs had infiltrated his normal language and conversations. Through his intellectual isolation and absorption in magic he had unwittingly allowed a mental corruption to take place. Whereas Jacobi had the willpower to separate himself from the magic by a massive effort, one got the feeling that magic had seeped into the soul of Wood's Prospero.

In these productions Prospero's motivation was also markedly different. This was clearly demonstrated in his relationship with Miranda. Closeness between father and daughter was established very early on in the 1988 production:

> In the scene where he relates to Miranda the tale of the overthrow of his Dukedom, Wood vacillates between tearful, frustrated anger ... and a touching need for emotional reassurance from his daughter.[52]

This Prospero was not only very affectionate to Miranda, but also relied on her to keep him emotionally grounded. His magical plot was orchestrated entirely for his daughter's future happiness:

> More maternal than fatherly this is a Prospero who practises not a 'rough magic' but a gentle magic ... when Prospero claims that all he has done is motivated by care for Miranda it is convincing.[53]

Jacobi, on the other hand, was quick to anger with his Miranda. Like a bad-tempered father he tolerated her interruptions, but ultimately she was a distraction from his magic. 'He is a man who has clearly been deposed in his prime and is willing every demon in nature to extract his revenge.'[54] Many reviewers felt he sailed close to losing the underlying humanity of the character: 'his wrath is so turbulent that we can never believe that he is as genuine in those moments of compassion which show us the other side of Prospero'.[55] By the end of the play, this Prospero's overarching motive was to re-establish himself in the Dukedom of Milan. John Wood, in the later production, by contrast, offered the very antithesis of this:

> Facing the Neapolitan court, Wood is almost unendurably pathetic .... With his book buried, Prospero has once more become a failed elder statesman, who may be permitted to return from exile because he no longer poses a threat. Awoken from the dream, the fantasy evaporating, *The Tempest* is proven to be Prospero's tragedy.[56]

The role of Prospero remains one of the great challenges for major actors. Having played the part in America many years before,

Patrick Stewart returned to it for the RSC in 2006, and in so doing proved that television and movie work (and fame) does not necessarily ruin an actor's ability to perform in the theatre. His appearance was described as reminiscent of 'some kind of shabby Lapland shaman, clad in a bearskin cloak and reindeer-skull headdress, raising the spirits from a burning brazier'.[57] His performance imbued the part with depth and humanity:

> Stewart proceeds to give a fine performance. True, you feel he's fibbing when he says that as duke of Milan he preferred books to politics, but he catches what really matters. Here's a Prospero with fierce feelings – doting father, bullying slave-master, proud magus, angry avenger – and the power to exercise them absolutely. Yet in the end he sacrifices control, accepts his own humanity, renounces revenge and, despite having captured the men who exiled him, forgives them.[58]

Caliban and Ariel on Stage

When researching the part of Caliban for the RSC's 1978 production, David Suchet made a startling discovery:

> imagine my horror when I discovered that Caliban had been played as: (1) a fish, (2) a dog with one and/or two heads, (3) a lizard, (4) a monkey, (5) a snake, (6) half-ape, half-man, with fins for arms, (7) a tortoise. These were just a few of the extreme interpretations. I, once again, began to feel rather depressed but I did manage a smile when I read that, when Caliban had been portrayed as a tortoise, Prospero would turn him on his back when he became unruly.[59]

Ariel and Caliban have been adapted to fit a multitude of different physical representations. The stage relationship between Prospero and these amorphous creatures has driven, and been driven by, twentieth-century critical interpretations of the play, whether it be Darwinian, Freudian or colonial. The outdated Darwinian reading that Suchet hints at above has all but become extinct. However,

Freudian interpretations continue, presenting Ariel and Caliban as elementals conjured from Prospero's subconscious. In Adrian Noble's 1998 production this was indicated through costume design:

> Scott Handy's sweet-voiced Ariel and Robert Glenister's anguished Caliban look like positive and negative photographic images of each other, both dressed in unflattering loin cloths, the one covered in white body-paint, the other in black slime. There is the suggestion that they are different aspects of Prospero's psyche, the super ego and the id perhaps.[60]

In many productions the costumes of Ariel and Caliban are designed to link in with Prospero's own attire. In one sense, there is the practical idea of Prospero clothing the natives to so called civilized standards with his cast-offs. But, for the audience it creates a physical and psychological link between the characters, where 'in its most reductive form, Ariel is his superego, [and] Caliban his libido'.

To increase the dramatic tension in the play, the majority of productions performed in the last fifty years have chosen to have a male actor play Ariel. 'From the eighteenth century until well into the twentieth, the part of Ariel was a coveted female role ... the cultural significance of gender and changing attitudes towards the power relationships in the play'[61] account for this shift in casting. Subjecting one man to the servitude of another automatically creates a tension, a power struggle that results in resentful servitude. Prospero, as a result, becomes an isolated figure, constantly at odds with those who wish him to relinquish his power over them. In the 1993 production Alec McCowen's Prospero could not

> afford to be complacent. Although he succeeds in controlling his world, his magic needs to be 'rough' because in addition to a thuggish Ariel, he has to control a terrifying Caliban and an unusually outspoken daughter. His wand doubles as a stick.[62]

In the first half of the twentieth century it was still common to portray Ariel and Caliban as the antithesis of each other, opposites in size, sex, attitude and colour – Ariel as loyal female, a white creature of the air, happy to please her master; Caliban as resentful subversive male, dark and earthy. The casting of men in these roles encouraged a parallel between Ariel and Caliban and their relationship with Prospero.

In the past fifty years the portrayal of Caliban evolved from a comic grotesque characterization of a missing link, to the 'noble savage'. David Suchet was memorable as Caliban in 1978 when he played the role sympathetically:

> Modern convention dictates that Caliban must be a sympathetic emblem of imperialistic exploitation, and that is how he is played here: a noble black innocent of magnificent physique speaking the language with the too-perfect precision of an alien.[63]

In Suchet's words, 'the monster was in the eyes of the beholder'.[64] Caliban's monstrosity was not attributed to deformity or from being an animalistic hybrid, but centred on his 'otherness':

> We must look seriously at how we in the western world perceive the 'other' – how we relate to it and how we talk about it in terms of ourselves. The whole sense of Caliban being taught language is cultural. Caliban is 'the other' and Prospero has power over him through language.[65]

Caliban's otherness is often represented by his colour (in 1974, Jeffery Kissoon played the part in The Other Place as 'a slave simply because of his colour'[66]). In Michael Boyd's 2002 production, Geff Francis was the first black actor to play the part on the RSC's main stage (previous white actors had blacked up when they confronted the issue). This reading of Caliban took the issue of colonialism and race head-on:

> His gabardine is an impressive garment, suggesting the rather worn cloak of a tribal chieftain very much in keeping with the production's emphasis on his dispossession.[67]

> Boyd makes sure that we spot the colonial problems that arise in this exotic realm. Malcolm Storry's white sweaty Prospero is domineering towards Kananu Kirimi's black, implicitly abused Ariel while Geff Francis's cruelly enslaved (and also black) Caliban pointedly cries more than once, 'This island's mine'. The ex-pat Europeans can certainly seem less civilised than the

natives, as Simon Gregor's upstart Trinculo makes entertainingly clear, reeling around like a drunk chimpanzee.[68]

The casting in this production of *The Tempest* pulled together a multitude of threads and issues that have dominated the portrayal of these characters for the last century. Kananu Kirimi was the first woman to play Ariel on the main stage at Stratford since 1952. In 1970 and in 1988 the director Jonathan Miller used black actors in the parts, but this production, which cast a black actress as Ariel, opened up a 'chance to explore parallels between colonisation of blacks by whites and of women by men'.[69] Caliban and Ariel were described as 'Caribbeans, seduced and exploited by Malcolm Storry's commanding Prospero'.[70] It brought to *The Tempest* the politics of gender and race prevalent in contemporary criticism:

> Throughout, the production shows how the urge to power can turn a paradise into a hell. In his harness and metal slave collar, Geff Francis's dignified and moving Caliban (who speaks the most haunting poetry in the play) is clearly a man more sinned against than sinning, and at the end, as Prospero begs the audience to set him free, the manacled Caliban remains, like a lingering rebuke to his cruel master.[71]

At the end of the play Prospero acknowledges responsibility for the damage he has done. Frankenstein-like, his rejection of this prodigious being as 'human' and his subsequent neglect awakens the 'monster' in Caliban. Instead of nurturing what he doesn't understand, and raising Caliban as he would his own child, he identifies him as something 'other'. Prospero's harsh treatment breeds resentment, anger, outrage and frustration to such a degree that Caliban plots his murder – avenging the man who usurped him as ruler of the isle.

In Sam Mendes' 1993 production, Ariel's vitriol was equal to Caliban's. His dominant command of the island's magic weakened Alec McCowen's impact as Prospero, and made Ariel the more imposing figure:

> In our production we had a very interesting portrayal of Ariel. Simon Russell Beale doesn't really look like an 'airy spirit': he was

more of an equal, which made Prospero's impatience and fury
with him all the more justified and understandable. I think when
Prospero screams and shouts at an Ariel played by a wispy little
(sometimes feminine) person or a child, it makes him appear
impossibly bullying.[72]

The watchful stillness of Simon Russell Beale's blue, Mao-suited
Ariel holds the dangerous tension of a coiled spring as its energy
is about to be liberated; the ticking of a time-bomb whose
moment is about to come. Held by silken bonds of gratitude and
the exercise of a power different from, but no greater than, his
own, he performs the tasks Prospero sets him with meticulous
ease and a hint of contempt at their largely trumpery nature.[73]

The positioning of this Ariel at the centre of the stage in the first
scene, controlling the magic of Prospero's storm, was unusual. His
power was depicted as equal to Prospero's, leading to a very strained
tension between master and servant. Reviewers talk of Ariel's barely
concealed hatred.

Prospero's last action is the release of Ariel. This moment can
express a close, friendly relationship between master and servant.
But it can also convey Ariel's impatience at the prospect of his
liberty. Thus, Mark Rylance's Ariel had already gone when Prospero
spoke the words which were supposed to release him. Sam Mendes
offered a startling revision of the entire relationship between
Prospero and Ariel. The previously unemotional, efficient servant
turned to Prospero and, spitting in his face, released the hatred and
disgust accumulated during the twelve years of his servitude. The
subsequent epilogue for Alec McCowen became the painful, weary
recognition of his project's failure and a true prayer for pardon and
relief from the 'good hands' of the audience.

The Inexhaustible *Tempest*

The Tempest seems to be inexhaustible. Clifford Williams' pessimistic
view of the play was criticized in 1963, but prefigured interpretations to come:

In this play Shakespeare includes all the themes from his earlier work – kingship, inheritance, treachery, conscience, identity, love, music, God; he draws them together as if to find the key to it all, but there is no such key. There is no grand order and Prospero returns to Milan not bathed in tranquillity, but a wreck.[74]

For Sam Mendes, 'The Tempest is, among other things about politics in a profound sense: moral and social order in human society. Who commands and why? Who obeys and why?'[75] 'In [Michael] Boyd's hands, this movingly becomes a play about the acquisition of grace and self-knowledge.'[76] David Thacker believes that 'The Tempest is an autobiographical play ... in which Shakespeare is dealing with the nature of his artistic achievement and the need to give up writing.'[77] To James McDonald,

It's a tempest of the mind ... shaped by people getting rid of extremes of emotion of grief and madness. And from that, rebirth can come ... [it] is about a number of huge opposites: drowning and rebirth, freedom and slavery, revenge and forgiveness, nature and nurture, sleeping and waking, seeming and being. An issue like colonialism is in there, but it's not all that the play's about .... Prospero ... has to learn to forgive people for the wrongs they have done. And that's a very difficult thing to do.[78]

THE DIRECTOR'S CUT: INTERVIEWS WITH PETER BROOK, SAM MENDES AND RUPERT GOOLD

Peter Brook (PB) is the most revered director of the second half of the twentieth century in the English-speaking world. Born in 1925, he first directed at Stratford in 1947. His work has been influenced by a range of approaches from Antonin Artaud's 'theatre of cruelty' and Jerzy Grotowski's 'poor theatre' to Indian and African notions of story-telling; The Empty Space, his book of 1968, remains the best introduction to his art. Following his groundbreaking 1970 'white box and circus skills' Midsummer Night's Dream at Stratford, he moved to Paris and founded his International Centre for Theatre

Research. He continued to produce innovative work at his intimate Bouffes du Nord Theatre well into his eighties. He has directed *The Tempest* no fewer than four times: in 1957, with John Gielgud as Prospero, again in 1963 and 1968, then in 1990 with his company of international actors at the Bouffes. In this interview, he speaks mostly about the last of these productions.

Sam Mendes (SM) was born in 1965 and began directing classic drama both for the RSC and on the West End stage soon after his graduation from Cambridge University. In the 1990s, he was artistic director of the intimate Donmar Warehouse in London. His first movie, *American Beauty* (1999), won Oscars for both Best Picture and Best Director. His 1993 RSC production of *The Tempest*, which he talks about here, featured Alec McCowen as Prospero and Simon Russell Beale as Ariel.

Rupert Goold (RG) was born in 1977. He studied at Cambridge and was an assistant director at the Donmar under Mendes. After undertaking a range of experimental work, he directed two highly acclaimed Shakespearean productions with the veteran stage and television actor Patrick Stewart: *The Tempest* of 2006, which he talks about here, part of the RSC's year-long Complete Works Festival, and an intimate *Macbeth* in 2007 at the Minerva Theatre, Chichester, with a transfer to London's West End.

The storm offers a spectacular opening to the play. How did you approach it from a design point of view?

PB: The first scene of *The Tempest* needs to be a beginning, leading one into the story. If it becomes a show in itself, the play cannot survive. Once, I staged it experimentally around a swinging plank, covered with bricks, with a model galleon in the middle. The actors stood behind and played the text – for once every word was heard! Then Prospero took a brick and smashed the ship. At once, Miranda cried out her protest and the story began. Then, when we did the play at the Bouffes, Ariel carried the model boat on his head, rocking a long tube full of pebbles to evoke the sound of waves as it was rocked and the actors held sticks to suggest the movements of the sea. This led straight into the scene between Prospero and Miranda – and the audience wanted to know more.

SM: The way I approached the storm was tied into my whole approach to the play. I would say that my production explored the play along lines that, crudely put, see Prospero as a director and his subjects as actors, and the journey of the play as an enactment created by Prospero in an empty space in order to lead to what he hopes will be ultimate resolution. My sense of the production now is that it was what I would call a young man's vision of the play. It was full of ideas and probably quite imaginative but not entirely rigorous in its thought process! It's a play that I'd love to do again and would now do quite differently.

The storm came out of the central conceit of the production, which is that Prospero had been washed up on the island with certain objects and they resided on his makeshift, driftwood desk throughout the production. There was a book that opened up into a Pollock's toy theatre, there was a vase of flowers, there was a small skip with his clothes, and out of those simple objects emerged all the magic and the poetry of the play. When the Lords, Gonzalo, Antonio, etc., arrived on the island for the first time they were surrounded by the flowers; to create the masque Ariel (played by Simon Russell Beale), opened the small Pollock's toy theatre book and a fully grown Pollock's toy theatre emerged out of the ground. Caliban's cave was Prospero's skip, and so on. So everything had a root in Prospero's belongings and the storm was no different.

The storm was created out of a skip and a swinging lantern. We began on an empty stage and the first image that you saw was Ariel walking up onto stage and swinging the lantern, and the moment the lantern went into motion the sailors exploded out of the skip and the stage became the boat. It was a deliberately theatrical conceit and at no point, like the rest of the production, attempted to convey the sense that the island was real. The island was a state of mind, a space in which Prospero could conduct his human experiment; his fantasy of revenge. There were photos in the programme of a variety of mad film directors, from Orson Welles to David Lean, who had tried to govern the natural world, to impose their will on it. That was our vision of Prospero.

RG: My starting point was in trying to convey the helpless fear one feels as a passenger when a storm hits – after all, most of the characters who speak in the scene are not mariners. Initially I intended to stage the scene on a plane during a crash as I expect most modern audiences will have more vivid and unsettling experiences of air travel than sea now. However, I worried that we would suffer in comparison to the TV series *Lost* (itself inspired by *The Tempest*) and so we stayed on a boat.

As a child I remember being on cross-channel ferries and feeling very vulnerable and it struck me that the experience below deck is more frightening than above. Perhaps our collective fear of burial alive has been stoked by submarine films but certainly that seemed an unusual focus. So Giles Cadle (our designer) and I tried to create a very claustrophobic navigation cell below deck into which the lords and mariners would pitch and panic. The idea of that cell being set in a radio came from my interest in opening with the shipping forecast and a rather weak pun on the word Ariel!

Perhaps what animated the sequence most in the end, though, were our queasy monumental projections of the pitching sea that accompanied the sequence.

There is an unusually long exposition in Act 1 scene 2, in which Prospero, as 'schoolmaster', narrates past events to Miranda, Ariel and Caliban. On one occasion, Miranda appears to be falling asleep – how did you avoid the risk that some audience members might join her?

PB: It's only if the storm is too spectacular that Prospero's tale becomes a bore. Yet when Gielgud played it – or on another occasion I saw Paul Scofield in the same role – it couldn't occur to anyone in the audience, nor even to the actors themselves, that this extraordinary narrative could be less than fascinating. But as Miranda has been brought up in an exotic dream, she has no living associations to connect to in this tale from another reality.

SM: It's called good acting! But I also gave Alec McCowen (who played Prospero) a little help: the people that he described walked on stage as he told his story. They emerged from behind a tiny screen, which was one of the other things that had been washed up on the island with him. It was used throughout the production to conjure up people centre-stage. The actors didn't make entrances and exits from the wings, they tended to emerge from behind objects – in this case, from behind the screen stepped all the people that Prospero was talking about, from Antonio to Gonzalo, so we animated his story a little.

I think that Shakespeare begins the play with a very simple story quite deliberately. A good actor will make an audience feel like they're sitting at his feet, very much like Miranda is, and will be as gripped by the story as she appears to be. Your reading of it is that she seems to be falling asleep. But I think Prospero is distracted – when he says 'Does thou hear', I think he is so wrapped up in his memories that he gradually becomes less and less aware of her as an audience. I don't think he's scrutinizing her for responses all the time. I think that having not talked about it for twelve years, he reopens old wounds, and is now plunged right back into the events themselves. I think that's the sort of thing that Shakespeare was after.

RG: I always wanted to not 'stage' the scene around Prospero and Miranda as some productions do, because unless you focus on Prospero's relationship to the story we never really get let in on him as a character. The idea we worked with was that although Prospero knew that the day of the play lay under 'an auspicious star', perhaps he didn't know what was going to be auspicious about it. Patrick [Stewart, who played Prospero] liked the idea that Prospero had been standing on the cliffs and seen the Neapolitan boat and, in that moment, decided to raise the storm. So he began the scene in a state of great agitation and shock and this gave it a useful urgency. I also think there are a lot of laughs in the scene if played properly, both in the text – Miranda's interjections mostly – but also in the relationship: the cranky old father/teacher and his trusting pupil.

The laughs and the rage, from both characters, shape the scene and prevent one long serene narration.

Neither Ariel nor Caliban is conventionally human: what particular challenges does the presence of such parts create for the director and the actor?

PB: In the Bouffes production, which was our most developed version after many years of trials and errors, I tried to avoid the clichés of a lighter-than-air dancer like Ariel – instead we had an African actor, Bakary Sangary, with the physique of a rugby player, but with such a lightness of spirit, wit and fantasy that he suggested Arielness more than any illustration could do. It was the same principle that had once led to acrobatics and dexterity for fairies in the *Midsummer Night's Dream*. With Caliban again we tried to avoid illustration – he was played by David Bennent, the same actor who had been the violent child in the film of Gunther Grass' *Tin Drum*. He suggested all the fury and rebellion of an adolescent in his relationship with the tyrannical adult who had power over him.

SM: Fun challenges! That's the joy of doing the play, how you render the other worlds that Prospero is attempting to control: the spiritual, the world of the air, and the earth. How do you render 'this thing of darkness / I acknowledge mine'? To me, that's one of the chief interpretative decisions that you have to make. How do you treat those figures? Do you treat them, as Peter Brook did, as totally and unexpectedly opposite figures, or, as Jonathan Miller has done, as two versions of the same thing – in Jonathan's case, enslaved natives. I felt like I had seen enough barnacled Rastafarian hunchbacked Calibans to last me a lifetime. I felt like the sense in which he is the beating heart of the play was diminished by making him merely a put-upon native. David Troughton and I wanted to keep him very, very simple, and all we ended up with was a single claw-like hand, and a very pale, hairless body. In the end I felt he was absolutely wonderful in the part and incredibly touching.

Simon Russell Beale's performance was in a way the most remarkable. Again we started off with a series of theatrical conceits we were going to attempt and abandoned them one after the other as we progressed. I sometimes think that's the true process of rehearsals – stripping away idea after idea, leaving one simple, beautiful one and that's what happened here. He was going to have a doll face, he was going to have some strange wig, he was going to wear white gloves and slippers, and it ended up as simply him in a blue Chairman Mao suit. He was a remarkably cold and restrained Ariel. You sensed always that there was a vast world that he was giving you only the merest glimpse of. Everything he did was in order to fulfil his obligations to Prospero and nothing more. When he appeared to be happy, it was exactly that, appearing to be happy, a pretence of happiness, a performance of happiness in order to become free again.

RG: The greatest problem is simply where to start. How can I be 'other' when my references are all human? I do think our Arctic context gave both actors a useful framework to work with though. Caliban's 'fishiness' worked well with a sort of seal-skin-wearing semi-Inuit, and John Light and I watched a couple of wonderful Inuit films which gave us both physical and spiritual entry points.

For Ariel I really wanted the production to find something truly terrifying and threatening. I was very interested in the relationship between *Dr Faustus* and *The Tempest*: two god-defying magicians – one who drowns his book, the other who screams 'I'll burn my books' but at the moment of his damnation when it is too late. The textual and thematic resonances are fascinating and I think I was equally intrigued by a Mephistophelean Ariel. A spirit who is the agent of the magic but also the source of the magician's power.

Literary critics and cultural historians have become particularly interested in *The Tempest* in relation to the dynamics of imperialism, colonial history and race: did you make a conscious effort to address these concerns in your research for, and rehearsal of, the play?

PB: It's too easy to slap simplistic politics onto Shakespeare. There was a time when military uniforms and references to colonialism

4. Prospero (Alec McCowen), defiant Ariel in 'Chairman Mao' suit (Simon Russell Beale) and sleeping Miranda (Sarah Woodward) in Act 1 scene 2 of Sam Mendes' 1993 RSC production.

refreshed the old Shakespeare imagery – today one must think again. The relationships are eternal; they, too, don't need to be illustrated by over-used clichés.

SM: I think that the more I study the play the more I agree with the cultural historians that it is in some part a discourse on race and slavery and you can't ignore that. However, I didn't focus on that in this production because I felt like that had been very well explored and other things interested me more. In large part one's own production of the play is part of a cultural history, and the question 'Is this at root a piece of colonial discourse?' had just been asked the year before by Jonathan Miller's production. To say it again was not very interesting. So you do become, to a degree, a victim of timing.

But directing *The Tempest* forces a personal response, as it's simply impossible to tick all the boxes. It is one of the most bottomless, unfathomable and profoundly mysterious plays ever written in the English language. Written towards the end of his life, it might be about elements of Shakespeare himself, might be about colonialism. Ted Hughes makes an incredibly strong point about how it is the concluding passage of Shakespeare's obsession with the Boar, rooted in Dido and Aeneas, and images that haunt him throughout his career, and when you read that you think 'Well of course that's what the play's about.'

And then how do you account for the masque? Is the play itself a masque? Peter Hall in his first production with John Gielgud played it absolutely straight down the line as a masque and that is fully justified also. There are many, many ways of interpreting this play and that is why it continues to be done. I think the job of the director is to relish and embrace the very personal nature of his response and not try and make a production that pleases all. I don't think with a play like this that that is possible. It pushes you to make choices and that is what is thrilling about it. It is also why a lot of directors – for example, Peter Hall and Peter Brook – have returned to the play more than once. It is one of those plays that reflects your state of mind when you are doing it.

I was thinking about doing the play again and did some research on it. I stumbled on descriptions of my own production and it was as alien to me as other people's productions. I thought, 'Wow, did I really do that?' There were photographs of it and I couldn't remember where it had come from. I think that is one of the wonderful gifts of this play. It is a Chinese box of a play. 'Infinite riches in a little room', in Christopher Marlowe's phrase [in *The Jew of Malta*]. It really is the most haiku-like of his plays. There aren't very many signs pointing the way for you and that's its glorious strength and its challenge.

RG: Not at a racial level. I suppose I felt the play had become a vessel for post-colonial readings through the twentieth century and that this was always liable to compromise the ethereal sense of magic in the play. Caliban and Ariel are, after all, magical creatures. That said, the idea of the Arctic – a shifting, evaporating, oft-claimed but never owned environment – did interest me. That just as

Prospero's vengeance melts away; so maybe does his island, and so the equating of territory with conflict became metaphorical.

When Gonzalo talks about the 'golden age' and how he would govern the isle, he is teased by the other characters: do you think it's essential that he should be regarded by the audience as a man of great dignity, a kind of moral centre, or can we share in the mockery?

PB: Gonzalo: always in Shakespeare opposites co-exist. The man of peace has an ideal, it needs to be felt as real – and at the same time he is completely out of touch with reality. So he's both touching and comic, like so many well meaning dreamers.

SM: I think as always with a Shakespeare play that both are true. At times he's a boring old buffoon. Yet he's a very, very kind man who has saved Prospero. I think it's dangerous to make him merely one or the other. In that respect it's a three-dimensional portrait.

RG: Both, surely. The jokes are funny and should be, as should Gonzalo's optimism in the face of catastrophe, but I think his handling of Alonso in particular shows a very shrewd and sensitive man.

Conversely, are Stephano and Trinculo just drunken clowns, or is there more to their role in the drama?

PB: Stephano, Trinculo and the plot to murder Prospero are a vital part of the dark underworld of the play which must be there to balance its fun, charm and lightness.

SM: I think Jan Kott [in his classic study *Shakespeare our Contemporary*] makes the point that they are a distorted version of the central story of the play. They play out a vaudevillian version of the king-making central plot. You get a sense of the sub-plot echoing the main plot, parodying those other characters. It also allows us to review the central plot, when we return to it, with greater clarity. So their purpose in the play is important. If you took them out of the play it would actually destroy it, because what they do in unlocking

Caliban and making him aware of the 'glories of drink' has a lot to do with one's understanding of the nature of master–servant relationships and what 'freedom' means.

With the subject, I tried to push that sense in which no one is ever fully able to control their subjects a little further. I made Trinculo (played by David Bradley) into a ventriloquist with a dummy dressed exactly like he was. When Ariel possesses Trinculo and makes him speak with Prospero's voice he possessed his ventriloquist's dummy instead. So again there was another version of the master unable to control his subject or the director unable to control his actors theme. We explored that to great length, particularly with Ariel. How nobody is a willing subject. Ultimately there is no such thing as a person who doesn't want on some level to control their own life and therefore to hold power. In that respect, going back to your earlier question, Gonzalo becomes a sort of a hero because he's the only person in the play who is willingly a subject.

RG: The clowns are very hard because they arrive so late and the gabardine sequence is so bloody difficult and so vaudeville. However, their second scene is, I think, the best in the play. The way the violence shifts between them and infects Caliban is extraordinarily rich. We always called it the 'Jamie Bulger' scene as the horrifying scenario of two bullying infant thugs leading a confused Caliban on a journey of violence seemed very familiar.

The text is explicit that Miranda is fifteen years old: what were the consequences of that for your production?

PB: We looked for the youngest girls we could find – in the end we had two of roughly the right age.

SM: I wanted someone who had a little bit more stage presence. When you are on a big stage, casting someone who is genuinely a girl doesn't always work. I think traditionally Mirandas fall into two categories: the tomboy Miranda who has taken after her father because the only thing she has ever known is the company of men; and the more feminine Miranda whose burgeoning sexuality is something that Prospero is increasingly mystified by but keenly feels the approach of.

The sexual jealousy of Prospero, and the tension between his wanting to give Miranda to Ferdinand and his wanting to retain her, is actually one of the best reasons to cast her at the age that she is supposed to be, and that may be one reason why Shakespeare is so explicit about her age. But I went for somebody who was already moving towards womanhood and had left her father behind, partly because I was interested in working with Sarah Woodward again, who could carry off some of the stridency of the role without losing sympathy. Also partly because Sarah makes me laugh and I think Miranda is actually a very funny part. She has the biggest laugh of the evening with 'O, wonder! / How many goodly creatures are there here!'

RG: We looked at what happens to girls who are brought up by their fathers alone. In the eighties there was a rash of girl prodigies, taught by ambitious fathers at home, going to Oxford at about the same age who all were hugely developed intellectually but retarded socially and sexually. We brought a child psychologist in who guided us on this but perhaps the greatest question any actor must answer is what has happened in the claimed rape story with Caliban. We developed quite a complex back-story around Miranda's first menstruation, and both Caliban and Prospero's response to it, to create a terrible event that all three of them had no real understanding of or ability to deal with.

What did your production infer from Antonio's silence in the face of Prospero's forgiveness of him?

PB: Quite rightly, he had nothing to say.

SM: He was unforgiven and unforgiving. The production had an unresolved, ambivalent ending on all fronts. There was nothing that went exactly as Prospero had planned it.

RG: That the feeling was not mutual. Of course it can be played as an expression of guilt but our whole approach to Act 5 was one of bathos. Prospero expects a great reconciliation but most of the lords treat him with a suspicion and hostility that is only interrupted by Miranda, Ferdinand and the clowns. We played all of Act 5 as a messy, frustrating, failure for Prospero, partly because we wanted to

5. Prospero (John Gielgud) in command over a cowering Ariel (Brian Bedford) in Peter Brook's production at the Shakespeare Memorial Theatre in 1957.

present the epilogue in as bleak and desolate a way as possible. A man with no answers, friends or powers. As such, a brother whose hatred is still explicit seemed the most useful.

John Gielgud said that the one thing he did consistently as Prospero in the four different productions in which he played the part over more than forty years was never to look Ariel directly in the face. With what sort of emotions did Prospero and Ariel part from each other in your production?

PB: John Gielgud made history at the time by playing Prospero clean-shaven. He also showed his violent anger. The play is called *The Tempest* not because of a noisy first scene, but because peace and calm, inner and outer only come at the very end when Prospero has managed to overcome his anger, his wish for revenge and his need for power. Until then, deep in his nature he remains Antonio's blood brother – the tempest is everywhere. As for emotions, the question is absurd. You don't define them, you play them.

SM: When Ariel was finally released he vented his spleen on Prospero and famously, I suppose now, spat in his face. That was the most controversial aspect of the production, but it felt absolutely earned and justified in his reading of the role. It was quite exciting to be in the Royal Shakespeare Theatre and to have people shout out. I watched a performance and two people shouted out 'Rubbish!' when he spat in his face. I rather liked it. It was an electric moment and it suddenly made you pity Prospero in a way that nothing else in the evening could have made you do. Suddenly he was the one who was lost. He has lost his powers and when he says 'Now my charms are all o'erthrown, / And what strength I have's mine own, / Which is most faint', it really meant something. He was talking in the moment. It didn't seem pre-planned. It seemed a response to what Ariel had just done to him. So to me that was a thrilling discovery. But it was entirely, as is often the case, due to a particular journey that I as the director and a group of actors had gone on. If I tried to impose it on another production, it wouldn't work at all. It was an organic thing that emerged out of rehearsals.

RG: Ariel only of release, a deep single sob of relief and annihilation. Prospero of confusion and sentiment – as one might release a treasured pet into the wild, hoping that he will look back but not really expecting it. This is all linked to the Act 5 reading I've outlined. Our Prospero wanted closure – with Miranda, Antonio, his magic, the island even – but life cannot be nicely stage-managed in the way he had hoped and, once emotions were let in, the ordered ending he had planned was in ruins.

What do you think was the hardest choice you had to make in creating your production of the play?

PB: I can never understand this word 'choice' which recurs constantly in Actor's Studio jargon. You certainly have to work hard and then in the end the choices make themselves by themselves.

SM: I think what is most difficult is how to realize the spiritual world. Unless you have a specific literal setting for the play, you have to render the spiritual world in a way that is convincing for a modern audience and feels real. The spectre of people in lycra with floaty pastel colours and net curtains rushing around pretending to be fairies is the thing that haunted me and I wanted to avoid. But that is also the reason that you do it. You do it because you don't have the answers to everything and because you are scared by the play and how impossible it appears. Those are the things that draw you to it. That's why I do what I do.

RG: Before we started the pre-production I went to see John Barton to get some insight – this was my first RSC Shakespeare and I figured I'd need all the help I could get. John told me the play was poor, one of Shakespeare's worst. That it could be done only two ways; either in the manner of Peter Brook, spare and ritualized, or as a big show with lots of effects and magic. He said the former never worked because it was just too portentous and dull and the plot was too silly to sustain such a reverent reading, and that the latter was just gaudy but at least had the virtue of the audiences enjoying it. He had directed the play at Stratford and seen forty years of productions and this was his considered conclusion on a play meant to be read not

6. Kananu Kirimi in Michael Boyd's 2002 production.

7. Julian Bleach as Ariel (*left*) in Rupert Goold's Arctic-set 2006 RSC production, designed by Giles Cadle, with costumes by Nicky Gillibrand.   8. Bakary Sangaré (*right*) as Ariel in *La Tempête*, directed by Peter Brook in 1990.

staged and knocked off quickly by a writer at the end of their career! The truth is that I'm afraid I rather agreed with him as I, too, had always found the lack of narrative energy, the absence of threat to Prospero and the general Robinson Crusoe atmosphere pretty dull in performance myself. I decided I would at least try and marry these 'holy' and spectacular elements – a staging that was theatrical and magical yet also hard-edged and cruel; one that could fill a large theatre and yet not become just a pageant. Of course, once you actually start work on any Shakespeare you can only see the million other choices you might have made and how rich and humbling his genius is. The hardest choice of all was in believing that we might ever succeed in doing the play justice.

SHAKESPEARE'S CAREER IN THE THEATRE

BEGINNINGS

William Shakespeare was an extraordinarily intelligent man who was born and died in an ordinary market town in the English Midlands. He lived an uneventful life in an eventful age. Born in April 1564, he was the eldest son of John Shakespeare, a glove-maker who was prominent on the town council until he fell into financial difficulties. Young William was educated at the local grammar in Stratford-upon-Avon, Warwickshire, where he gained a thorough grounding in the Latin language, the art of rhetoric and classical poetry. He married Ann Hathaway and had three children (Susanna, then the twins Hamnet and Judith) before his twenty-first birthday: an exceptionally young age for the period. We do not know how he supported his family in the mid-1580s.

Like many clever country boys, he moved to the city in order to make his way in the world. Like many creative people, he found a career in the entertainment business. Public playhouses and professional full-time acting companies reliant on the market for their income were born in Shakespeare's childhood. When he arrived in London as a man, sometime in the late 1580s, a new phenomenon was in the making: the actor who is so successful that he becomes a 'star'. The word did not exist in its modern sense, but the pattern is recognizable: audiences went to the theatre not so much to see a particular show as to witness the comedian Richard Tarlton or the dramatic actor Edward Alleyn.

Shakespeare was an actor before he was a writer. It appears not to have been long before he realized that he was never going to grow into a great comedian like Tarlton or a great tragedian like Alleyn.

Instead, he found a role within his company as the man who patched up old plays, breathing new life, new dramatic twists, into tired repertory pieces. He paid close attention to the work of the university-educated dramatists who were writing history plays and tragedies for the public stage in a style more ambitious, sweeping and poetically grand than anything which had been seen before. But he may also have noted that what his friend and rival Ben Jonson would call 'Marlowe's mighty line' sometimes faltered in the mode of comedy. Going to university, as Christopher Marlowe did, was all well and good for honing the arts of rhetorical elaboration and classical allusion, but it could lead to a loss of the common touch. To stay close to a large segment of the potential audience for public theatre, it was necessary to write for clowns as well as kings and to intersperse the flights of poetry with the humour of the tavern, the privy and the brothel: Shakespeare was the first to establish himself early in his career as an equal master of tragedy, comedy and history. He realized that theatre could be the medium to make the national past available to a wider audience than the elite who could afford to read large history books: his signature early works include not only the classical tragedy *Titus Andronicus* but also the sequence of English historical plays on the Wars of the Roses.

He also invented a new role for himself, that of in-house company dramatist. Where his peers and predecessors had to sell their plays to the theatre managers on a poorly-paid piecework basis, Shakespeare took a percentage of the box-office income. The Lord Chamberlain's Men constituted themselves in 1594 as a joint stock company, with the profits being distributed among the core actors who had invested as sharers. Shakespeare acted himself – he appears in the cast lists of some of Ben Jonson's plays as well as the list of actors' names at the beginning of his own collected works – but his principal duty was to write two or three plays a year for the company. By holding shares, he was effectively earning himself a royalty on his work, something no author had ever done before in England. When the Lord Chamberlain's Men collected their fee for performance at court in the Christmas season of 1594, three of them went along to the Treasurer of the Chamber: not just Richard

Burbage the tragedian and Will Kempe the clown, but also Shakespeare the scriptwriter. That was something new.

The next four years were the golden period in Shakespeare's career, though overshadowed by the death of his only son Hamnet, aged eleven, in 1596. In his early thirties and in full command of both his poetic and his theatrical medium, he perfected his art of comedy, while also developing his tragic and historical writing in new ways. In 1598, Francis Meres, a Cambridge University graduate with his finger on the pulse of the London literary world, praised Shakespeare for his excellence across the genres:

> As Plautus and Seneca are accounted the best for comedy and tragedy among the Latins, so Shakespeare among the English is the most excellent in both kinds for the stage; for comedy, witness his *Gentlemen of Verona*, his *Errors*, his *Love Labours Lost*, his *Love Labours Won*, his *Midsummer Night Dream* and his *Merchant of Venice*: for tragedy his *Richard the 2*, *Richard the 3*, *Henry the 4*, *King John*, *Titus Andronicus* and his *Romeo and Juliet*.

For Meres, as for the many writers who praised the 'honey-flowing vein' of *Venus and Adonis* and *Lucrece*, narrative poems written when the theatres were closed due to plague in 1593–94, Shakespeare was marked above all by his linguistic skill, by the gift of turning elegant poetic phrases.

PLAYHOUSES

Elizabethan playhouses were 'thrust' or 'one-room' theatres. To understand Shakespeare's original theatrical life, we have to forget about the indoor theatre of later times, with its proscenium arch and curtain that would be opened at the beginning and closed at the end of each act. In the proscenium arch theatre, stage and auditorium are effectively two separate rooms: the audience looks from one world into another as if through the imaginary 'fourth wall' framed by the proscenium. The picture-frame stage, together with the elaborate scenic effects and backdrops beyond it, created the illusion of a self-contained world – especially once nineteenth-century developments in the control of artificial lighting meant that the auditorium could be darkened and the spectators made to focus on the lighted stage. Shakespeare, by contrast, wrote for a bare platform stage with a standing audience gathered around it in a courtyard in full daylight. The audience were always conscious of themselves and their fellow-spectators, and they shared the same 'room' as the actors. A sense of immediate presence and the creation of rapport with the audience were all-important. The actor could not afford to imagine he was in a closed world, with silent witnesses dutifully observing him from the darkness.

Shakespeare's theatrical career began at the Rose Theatre in Southwark. The stage was wide and shallow, trapezoid in shape, like a lozenge. This design had a great deal of potential for the theatrical equivalent of cinematic split-screen effects, whereby one group of characters would enter at the door at one end of the tiring-house wall at the back of the stage and another group through the door at the other end, thus creating two rival tableaux. Many of the battle-heavy and faction-filled plays that premiered at the Rose have scenes of just this sort.

At the rear of the Rose stage, there were three capacious exits, each over ten feet wide. Unfortunately, the very limited excavation of a fragmentary portion of the original Globe site, also in 1989, revealed nothing about the stage. The first Globe was built in 1599 with similar proportions to those of another theatre, the Fortune, albeit that the former was polygonal and looked circular, whereas the latter was rectangular. The building contract for the Fortune survives and allows us to infer that the stage of the Globe was probably substantially wider than it was deep (perhaps forty-three feet wide and twenty-seven feet deep). It may well have been tapered at the front, like that of the Rose.

The capacity of the Globe was said to have been enormous, perhaps in excess of three thousand. It has been conjectured that about eight hundred people may have stood in the yard, with two thousand or more in the three layers of covered galleries. The other 'public' playhouses were also of large capacity, whereas the indoor Blackfriars theatre that Shakespeare's company began using in

1608 – the former refectory of a monastery – had overall internal dimensions of a mere forty-six by sixty feet. It would have made for a much more intimate theatrical experience and had a much smaller capacity, probably of about six hundred people. Since they paid at least sixpence a head, the Blackfriars attracted a more select or 'private' audience. The atmosphere would have been closer to that of an indoor performance before the court in the Whitehall Palace or at Richmond. That Shakespeare always wrote for indoor production at court as well as outdoor performance in the public theatre should make us cautious about inferring, as some scholars have, that the opportunity provided by the intimacy of the Blackfriars led to a significant change towards a 'chamber' style in his last plays – which, besides, were performed at both the Globe and the Blackfriars. After the occupation of the Blackfriars a five-act structure seems to have become more important to Shakespeare. That was because of artificial lighting: there were musical interludes between the acts, while the candles were trimmed and replaced. Again, though, something similar must have been necessary for indoor court performances throughout his career.

Front of house there were the 'gatherers' who collected the money from audience members: a penny to stand in the open-air yard, another penny for a place in the covered galleries, sixpence for the prominent 'lord's rooms' to the side of the stage. In the indoor 'private' theatres, gallants from the audience who fancied making themselves part of the spectacle sat on stools on the edge of the stage itself. Scholars debate as to how widespread this practice was in the public theatres such as the Globe. Once the audience were in place and the money counted, the gatherers were available to be extras on stage. That is one reason why battles and crowd scenes often come later rather than early in Shakespeare's plays. There was no formal prohibition upon performance by women, and there certainly were women among the gatherers, so it is not beyond the bounds of possibility that female crowd members were played by females.

The play began at two o'clock in the afternoon and the theatre had to be cleared by five. After the main show, there would be a jig – which consisted not only of dancing, but also of knockabout comedy (it is the origin of the farcical 'afterpiece' in the eighteenth-century theatre). So the time available for a Shakespeare play was about two and a half hours, somewhere between the 'two hours' traffic' mentioned in the prologue to *Romeo and Juliet* and the 'three hours' spectacle' referred to in the preface to the 1647 Folio of Beaumont and Fletcher's plays. The prologue to a play by Thomas Middleton refers to a thousand lines as 'one hour's words', so the likelihood is that about two and a half thousand, or a maximum of three thousand lines made up the performed text. This is indeed the length of most of Shakespeare's comedies, whereas many of his tragedies and histories are much longer, raising the possibility that he wrote full scripts, possibly with eventual publication in mind, in the full knowledge that the stage version would be heavily cut. The short Quarto texts published in his lifetime – they used to be called 'Bad' Quartos – provide fascinating evidence as to the kind of cutting that probably took place. So, for instance, the First Quarto of *Hamlet* neatly merges two occasions when Hamlet is overheard, the 'Fishmonger' and the 'nunnery' scenes.

The social composition of the audience was mixed. The poet Sir John Davies wrote of 'A thousand townsmen, gentlemen and whores, / Porters and servingmen' who would 'together throng' at the public playhouses. Though moralists associated female play-going with adultery and the sex trade, many perfectly respectable citizens' wives were regular attendees. Some, no doubt, resembled the modern groupie: a story attested in two different sources has one citizen's wife making a post-show assignation with Richard Burbage and ending up in bed with Shakespeare – supposedly eliciting from the latter the quip that William the Conqueror was before Richard III. Defenders of theatre liked to say that by witnessing the comeuppance of villains on the stage, audience members would repent of their own wrongdoings, but the reality is that most people went to the theatre then, as they do now, for entertainment more than moral edification. Besides, it would be foolish to suppose that audiences behaved in a homogeneous way: a pamphlet of the 1630s tells of how two men went to see *Pericles* and one of them laughed while the other wept. Bishop John Hall complained that people went to church for the same reasons that they went to the theatre: 'for company, for custom, for recreation ... to feed his eyes or his ears ... or perhaps for sleep'.

Men-about-town and clever young lawyers went to be seen as much as to see. In the modern popular imagination, shaped not least by *Shakespeare in Love* and the opening sequence of Laurence Olivier's *Henry V* film, the penny-paying groundlings stand in the yard hurling abuse or encouragement and hazelnuts or orange peel at the actors, while the sophisticates in the covered galleries appreciate Shakespeare's soaring poetry. The reality was probably the other way round. A 'groundling' was a kind of fish, so the nickname suggests the penny audience standing below the level of the stage and gazing in silent open-mouthed wonder at the spectacle unfolding above them. The more difficult audience members, who kept up a running commentary of clever remarks on the performance and who occasionally got into quarrels with players, were the gallants. Like Hollywood movies in modern times, Elizabethan and Jacobean plays exercised a powerful influence on the fashion and behaviour of the young. John Marston mocks the lawyers who would open their lips, perhaps to court a girl, and out would 'flow / Naught but pure Juliet and Romeo'.

THE ENSEMBLE AT WORK

In the absence of typewriters and photocopying machines, reading aloud would have been the means by which the company got to know a new play. The tradition of the playwright reading his complete script to the assembled company endured for generations. A copy would then have been taken to the Master of the Revels for licensing. The theatre book-holder or prompter would then have copied the parts for distribution to the actors. A partbook consisted of the character's lines, with each speech preceded by the last three or four words of the speech before, the so-called 'cue'. These would have been taken away and studied or 'conned'. During this period of learning the parts, an actor might have had some one-to-one instruction, perhaps from the dramatist, perhaps from a senior actor

9. Hypothetical reconstruction of the interior of an Elizabethan playhouse during a performance.

who had played the same part before, and, in the case of an apprentice, from his master. A high percentage of Desdemona's lines occur in dialogue with Othello, of Lady Macbeth's with Macbeth, Cleopatra's with Antony and Volumnia's with Coriolanus. The roles would almost certainly have been taken by the apprentice of the lead actor, usually Burbage, who delivers the majority of the cues. Given that apprentices lodged with their masters, there would have been ample opportunity for personal instruction, which may be what made it possible for young men to play such demanding parts.

After the parts were learned, there may have been no more than a single rehearsal before the first performance. With six different plays to be put on every week, there was no time for more. Actors, then, would go into a show with a very limited sense of the whole. The notion of a collective rehearsal process that is itself a process of discovery for the actors is wholly modern and would have been incomprehensible to Shakespeare and his original ensemble. Given the number of parts an actor had to hold in his memory, the forgetting of lines was probably more frequent than in the modern theatre. The book-holder was on hand to prompt.

Backstage personnel included the property man, the tire-man who oversaw the costumes, call-boys, attendants and the musicians, who might play at various times from the main stage, the rooms above and within the tiring-house. Scriptwriters sometimes made a nuisance of themselves backstage. There was often tension between the acting companies and the freelance playwrights from whom they purchased scripts: it was a smart move on the part of Shakespeare and the Lord Chamberlain's Men to bring the writing process in-house.

Scenery was limited, though sometimes set-pieces were brought on (a bank of flowers, a bed, the mouth of hell). The trapdoor from below, the gallery stage above and the curtained discovery-space at the back allowed for an array of special effects: the rising of ghosts and apparitions, the descent of gods, dialogue between a character at a window and another at ground level, the revelation of a statue or a pair of lovers playing at chess. Ingenious use could be made of props, as with the ass's head in *A Midsummer Night's Dream*. In a theatre that does not clutter the stage with the material paraphernalia of everyday life, those objects that are deployed may take on powerful symbolic weight, as when Shylock bears his weighing scales in one hand and knife in the other, thus becoming a parody of the figure of Justice who traditionally bears a sword and a balance. Among the more significant items in the property cupboard of Shakespeare's company, there would have been a throne (the 'chair of state'), joint stools, books, bottles, coins, purses, letters (which are brought on stage, read or referred to on about eighty occasions in the complete works), maps, gloves, a set of stocks (in which Kent is put in *King Lear*), rings, rapiers, daggers, broadswords, staves, pistols, masks and vizards, heads and skulls, torches and tapers and lanterns which served to signal night scenes on the daylit stage, a buck's head, an ass's head, animal costumes. Live animals also put in appearances, most notably the dog Crab in *The*

Two Gentlemen of Verona and possibly a young polar bear in *The Winter's Tale*.

The costumes were the most important visual dimension of the play. Playwrights were paid between £2 and £6 per script, whereas Alleyn was not averse to paying £20 for 'a black velvet cloak with sleeves embroidered all with silver and gold'. No matter the period of the play, actors always wore contemporary costume. The excitement for the audience came not from any impression of historical accuracy, but from the richness of the attire and perhaps the transgressive thrill of the knowledge that here were commoners like themselves strutting in the costumes of courtiers in effective defiance of the strict sumptuary laws whereby in real life people had to wear the clothes that befitted their social station.

To an even greater degree than props, costumes could carry symbolic importance. Racial characteristics could be suggested: a breastplate and helmet for a Roman soldier, a turban for a Turk, long robes for exotic characters such as Moors, a gabardine for a Jew. The figure of Time, as in *The Winter's Tale*, would be equipped with hourglass, scythe and wings; Rumour, who speaks the prologue of *2 Henry IV*, wore a costume adorned with a thousand tongues. The wardrobe in the tiring-house of the Globe would have contained much of the same stock as that of rival manager Philip Henslowe at the Rose: green gowns for outlaws and foresters, black for melancholy men such as Jaques and people in mourning such as the Countess in *All's Well that Ends Well* (at the beginning of *Hamlet*, the prince is still in mourning black when everyone else is in festive garb for the wedding of the new king), a gown and hood for a friar (or a feigned friar like the duke in *Measure for Measure*), blue coats and tawny to distinguish the followers of rival factions, a leather apron and ruler for a carpenter (as in the opening scene of *Julius Caesar* – and in *A Midsummer Night's Dream*, where this is the only sign that Peter Quince is a carpenter), a cockle hat with staff and a pair of sandals for a pilgrim or palmer (the disguise assumed by Helen in *All's Well*), bodices and kirtles with farthingales beneath for the boys who are to be dressed as girls. A gender switch such as that of Rosalind or Jessica seems to have taken between fifty and eighty lines of dialogue – Viola does not resume her 'maiden weeds', but remains in her boy's costume to the end of *Twelfth Night* because a change would have slowed down the action at just the moment it was speeding to a climax. Henslowe's inventory also included 'a robe for to go invisible': Oberon, Puck and Ariel must have had something similar.

As the costumes appealed to the eyes, so there was music for the ears. Comedies included many songs. Desdemona's willow song, perhaps a late addition to the text, is a rare and thus exceptionally poignant example from tragedy. Trumpets and tuckets sounded for ceremonial entrances, drums denoted an army on the march. Background music could create atmosphere, as at the beginning of *Twelfth Night*, during the lovers' dialogue near the end of *The Merchant of Venice*, when the statue seemingly comes to life in *The Winter's Tale*, and for the revival of Pericles and of Lear (in the Quarto text, but not the Folio). The haunting sound of the hautboy suggested a realm beyond the human, as when the god Hercules is imagined deserting Mark Antony. Dances symbolized the harmony of the end of a comedy – though in Shakespeare's world of mingled joy and sorrow, someone is usually left out of the circle.

The most important resource was, of course, the actors themselves. They needed many skills: in the words of one contemporary commentator, 'dancing, activity, music, song, elocution, ability of body, memory, skill of weapon, pregnancy of wit'. Their bodies were as significant as their voices. Hamlet tells the player to 'suit the action to the word, the word to the action': moments of strong emotion, known as 'passions', relied on a repertoire of dramatic gestures as well as a modulation of the voice. When Titus Andronicus has had his hand chopped off, he asks 'How can I grace my talk, / Wanting a hand to give it action?' A pen portrait of 'The Character of an Excellent Actor' by the dramatist John Webster is almost certainly based on his impression of Shakespeare's leading man, Richard Burbage: 'By a full and significant action of body, he charms our attention: sit in a full theatre, and you will think you see so many lines drawn from the circumference of so many ears, whiles the actor is the centre . . . .'

Though Burbage was admired above all others, praise was also heaped upon the apprentice players whose alto voices fitted them for the parts of women. A spectator at Oxford in 1610 records how the audience were reduced to tears by the pathos of Desdemona's death. The puritans who fumed about the biblical prohibition upon cross-dressing and the encouragement to sodomy constituted by the sight of an adult male kissing a teenage boy on stage were a small minority. Little is known, however, about the characteristics of the leading apprentices in Shakespeare's company. It may perhaps be inferred that one was a lot taller than the other, since Shakespeare often wrote for a pair of female friends, one tall and fair, the other short and dark (Helena and Hermia, Rosalind and Celia, Beatrice and Hero).

We know little about Shakespeare's own acting roles – an early allusion indicates that he often took royal parts, and a venerable tradition gives him old Adam in *As You Like It* and the ghost of old King Hamlet. Save for Burbage's lead roles and the generic part of the clown, all such castings are mere speculation. We do not even know for sure whether the original Falstaff was Will Kempe or another actor who specialized in comic roles, Thomas Pope.

Kempe left the company in early 1599. Tradition has it that he fell out with Shakespeare over the matter of excessive improvisation. He was replaced by Robert Armin, who was less of a clown and more of a cerebral wit: this explains the difference between such parts as Lancelet Gobbo and Dogberry, which were written for Kempe, and the more verbally sophisticated Feste and Lear's Fool, which were written for Armin.

One thing that is clear from surviving 'plots' or story-boards of plays from the period is that a degree of doubling was necessary. *2 Henry VI* has over sixty speaking parts, but more than half of the characters only appear in a single scene and most scenes have only six to eight speakers. At a stretch, the play could be performed by thirteen actors. When Thomas Platter saw *Julius Caesar* at the Globe in 1599, he noted that there were about fifteen. Why doesn't Paris go to the Capulet ball in *Romeo and Juliet*? Perhaps because he was doubled with Mercutio, who does. In *The Winter's Tale*, Mamillius might have come back as Perdita and Antigonus been doubled by Camillo, making the partnership with Paulina at the end a very neat touch. Titania and Oberon are often played by the same pair as Hippolyta and Theseus, suggesting a symbolic matching of the rulers of the worlds of night and day, but it is questionable whether there would have been time for the necessary costume changes. As so often, one is left in a realm of tantalizing speculation.

THE KING'S MAN

The new king, James I, who had held the Scottish throne as James VI since he had been an infant, immediately took the Lord Chamberlain's Men under his direct patronage. Henceforth they would be the King's Men, and for the rest of Shakespeare's career they were favoured with far more court performances than any of their rivals. There even seem to have been rumours early in the reign that Shakespeare and Burbage were being considered for knighthoods, an unprecedented honour for mere actors – and one that in the event was not accorded to a member of the profession for nearly three hundred years, when the title was bestowed upon Henry Irving, the leading Shakespearean actor of Queen Victoria's reign.

Shakespeare's productivity rate slowed in the Jacobean years, not because of age or some personal trauma, but because there were frequent outbreaks of plague, causing the theatres to be closed for long periods. The King's Men were forced to spend many months on the road. Between November 1603 and 1608, they were to be found at various towns in the south and Midlands, though Shakespeare probably did not tour with them by this time. He had bought a large house back home in Stratford and was accumulating other property. He may indeed have stopped acting soon after the new king took the throne. With the London theatres closed so much of the time and a large repertoire on the stocks, Shakespeare seems to have focused his energies on writing a few long and complex tragedies that could have been played on demand at court: *Othello, King Lear, Antony and Cleopatra, Coriolanus* and *Cymbeline* are among his longest and poetically grandest plays. *Macbeth* only survives in a shorter text, which shows signs of adaptation after Shakespeare's death. The bitterly satirical *Timon of Athens*, apparently a collaboration with Thomas Middleton that may have failed on the stage, also belongs to this period. In comedy, too, he wrote longer and morally darker works than in the Elizabethan period, pushing at the very bounds of the form in *Measure for Measure* and *All's Well that Ends Well*.

From 1608 onwards, when the King's Men began occupying the indoor Blackfriars playhouse (as a winter house, meaning that they only used the outdoor Globe in summer?), Shakespeare turned to a more romantic style. His company had a great success with a revived and altered version of an old pastoral play called *Mucedorus*. It even featured a bear. The younger dramatist John Fletcher, meanwhile, sometimes working in collaboration with Francis Beaumont, was pioneering a new style of tragicomedy, a mix of romance and royalism laced with intrigue and pastoral excursions. Shakespeare experimented with this idiom in *Cymbeline* and it was presumably with his blessing that Fletcher eventually took over as the King's Men's company dramatist. The two writers apparently collaborated on three plays in the years 1612–14: a lost romance called *Cardenio* (based on the love-madness of a character in Cervantes' *Don Quixote*), *Henry VIII* (originally staged with the title 'All is True'), and *The Two Noble Kinsmen*, a dramatization of Chaucer's 'Knight's Tale' These were written after Shakespeare's two final solo-authored plays, *The Winter's Tale*, a self-consciously old-fashioned work dramatizing the pastoral romance of his old enemy Robert Greene, and *The Tempest*, which at one and the same time drew together multiple theatrical traditions, diverse reading and contemporary interest in the fate of a ship that had been wrecked on the way to the New World.

The collaborations with Fletcher suggest that Shakespeare's career ended with a slow fade rather than the sudden retirement supposed by the nineteenth-century Romantic critics who read Prospero's epilogue to *The Tempest* as Shakespeare's personal farewell to his art. In the last few years of his life Shakespeare certainly spent more of his time in Stratford-upon-Avon, where he became further involved in property dealing and litigation. But his London life also continued. In 1613 he made his first major London property purchase: a freehold house in the Blackfriars district, close to his company's indoor theatre. *The Two Noble Kinsmen* may have been written as late as 1614, and Shakespeare was in London on business a little over a year before he died of an unknown cause at home in Stratford-upon-Avon in 1616, probably on his fifty-second birthday.

About half the sum of his works were published in his lifetime, in texts of variable quality. A few years after his death, his fellow-actors began putting together an authorized edition of his complete *Comedies, Histories and Tragedies*. It appeared in 1623, in large 'Folio' format. This collection of thirty-six plays gave Shakespeare his immortality. In the words of his fellow-dramatist Ben Jonson, who contributed two poems of praise at the start of the Folio, the body of his work made him 'a monument without a tomb':

And art alive still while thy book doth live
And we have wits to read and praise to give ...
He was not of an age, but for all time!

SHAKESPEARE'S WORKS: A CHRONOLOGY

1589–91	*? Arden of Faversham* (possible part authorship)
1589–92	*The Taming of the Shrew*
1589–92	*? Edward the Third* (possible part authorship)
1591	*The Second Part of Henry the Sixth*, originally called *The First Part of the Contention betwixt the Two Famous Houses of York and Lancaster* (element of co-authorship possible)
1591	*The Third Part of Henry the Sixth*, originally called *The True Tragedy of Richard Duke of York* (element of co-authorship probable)
1591–92	*The Two Gentlemen of Verona*
1591–92 perhaps revised 1594	*The Lamentable Tragedy of Titus Andronicus* (probably co-written with, or revising an earlier version by, George Peele)
1592	*The First Part of Henry the Sixth*, probably with Thomas Nashe and others
1592/94	*King Richard the Third*
1593	*Venus and Adonis* (poem)
1593–94	*The Rape of Lucrece* (poem)
1593–1608	*Sonnets* (154 poems, published 1609 with *A Lover's Complaint*, a poem of disputed authorship)
1592–94/ 1600–03	*Sir Thomas More* (a single scene for a play originally by Anthony Munday, with other revisions by Henry Chettle, Thomas Dekker and Thomas Heywood)
1594	*The Comedy of Errors*
1595	*Love's Labour's Lost*
1595–97	*Love's Labour's Won* (a lost play, unless the original

	title for another comedy)
1595–96	*A Midsummer Night's Dream*
1595–96	*The Tragedy of Romeo and Juliet*
1595–96	*King Richard the Second*
1595–97	*The Life and Death of King John* (possibly earlier)
1596–97	*The Merchant of Venice*
1596–97	*The First Part of Henry the Fourth*
1597–98	*The Second Part of Henry the Fourth*
1598	*Much Ado about Nothing*
1598–99	*The Passionate Pilgrim* (20 poems, some not by Shakespeare)
1599	*The Life of Henry the Fifth*
1599	'To the Queen' (epilogue for a court performance)
1599	*As You Like It*
1599	*The Tragedy of Julius Caesar*
1600–01	*The Tragedy of Hamlet, Prince of Denmark* (perhaps revising an earlier version)
1600–01	*The Merry Wives of Windsor* (perhaps revising version of 1597–99)
1601	'Let the Bird of Loudest Lay' (poem, known since 1807 as 'The Phoenix and Turtle' (turtle-dove))
1601	*Twelfth Night, or What You Will*
1601–02	*The Tragedy of Troilus and Cressida*
1604	*The Tragedy of Othello, the Moor of Venice*
1604	*Measure for Measure*
1605	*All's Well that Ends Well*
1605	*The Life of Timon of Athens*, with Thomas Middleton
1605–06	*The Tragedy of King Lear*
1605–08	? contribution to *The Four Plays in One* (lost, except for *A Yorkshire Tragedy*, mostly by Thomas Middleton)
1606	*The Tragedy of Macbeth* (surviving text has additional scenes by Thomas Middleton)
1606–07	*The Tragedy of Antony and Cleopatra*
1608	*The Tragedy of Coriolanus*
1608	*Pericles, Prince of Tyre*, with George Wilkins

1610	*The Tragedy of Cymbeline*
1611	*The Winter's Tale*
1611	*The Tempest*
1612–13	*Cardenio*, with John Fletcher (survives only in later adaptation called *Double Falsehood* by Lewis Theobald)
1613	*Henry VIII (All is True)*, with John Fletcher
1613–14	*The Two Noble Kinsmen*, with John Fletcher

FURTHER READING
AND VIEWING

CRITICAL APPROACHES

Bate, Jonathan, 'A Voice for Ariel', in his *The Song of the Earth* (2000), pp. 68–93. An ecological approach.

Berger, Harry Jr., 'Miraculous Harp: A Reading of Shakespeare's *Tempest*', *Shakespeare Studies* V (1969), pp. 253–83. A superb close reading.

Brower, Reuben A., 'The Mirror of Analogy' (1951) in *The Tempest: A Casebook*, ed. D. J. Palmer (1991), pp. 153–75. Close reading with classical context.

Brown, Paul, '"This Thing of Darkness I Acknowledge Mine": *The Tempest* and the Discourse of Colonialism', in *Political Shakespeare: New Essays in Cultural Materialism*, ed. Jonathan Dollimore and Alan Sinfield (1985), pp. 48–71. Self-consciously post-colonial approach.

Felperin, Howard, *Shakespearean Romance* (1972). Sophisticated sense of the slipperiness of the genre.

Gillies, John, 'Shakespeare's Virginian Masque', *ELH: A Journal of English Literary History*, 53 (1986), pp. 673–707. The 'brave new world' in historical context.

Hulme, Peter, and William Sherman, eds, *'The Tempest' and its Travels* (2000). Excellent collection of essays, covering post-colonial approaches and more.

Kermode, Frank, 'Introduction to *The Tempest*' (1954), in *The Tempest: A Casebook*, ed. D. J. Palmer (1991), pp. 151–67. On Prospero's white magic, and on nature and art, from classic introduction to old Arden edition.

Lamming, George, 'A Monster, a Child, a Slave', in his *Pleasures of Exile* (1960), pp. 95–117. View from a Caribbean-born writer.

Lindley, David, 'Music, Masque and Meaning in *The Tempest*', in his *The Court Masque* (1984), pp. 47–59. Very clear account of why music matters.

Nuttall, A. D., *Two Concepts of Allegory: A Study of Shakespeare's 'The Tempest' and the Logic of Allegorical Expression* (1967). Dazzling but demanding.

Orgel, Stephen, 'Prospero's Wife', *Representations*, 8 (1985), pp. 1–13. On questions of gender and a key absence.

Vaughan, Alden T., and Virginia Mason Vaughan, *Shakespeare's Caliban: A Cultural History* (1991). Fascinating material.

Wilson Knight, G., 'The Shakespearian Superman' (1947), in *The Tempest: A Casebook*, ed. D. J. Palmer (1991), pp. 111–30. Quasi-mystical, full of poetic insight.

THE PLAY IN PERFORMANCE

Brook, Peter, *The Empty Space* (1968). Perhaps the modern theatre's most influential director's manifesto.

Brooke, Michael, 'The Tempest on Screen', www.screenonline.org. uk/tv/id/564758/index.html. Valuable overview. Registered schools, colleges, universities and libraries have access to video clips, including the complete twelve minutes of the silent 1908 version.

Dymkowski, Christine, *The Tempest*, Shakespeare in Production (2000). Covers many key productions.

Greenaway, Peter, *Prospero's Books: A Film of Shakespeare's The Tempest* (1991). Screenplay.

Hirst, David, *The Tempest: Text and Performance* (1984). Good range.

Lindley, David, *The Tempest*, Shakespeare at Stratford (2003). RSC stagings and earlier ones.

RSC 'Exploring Shakespeare: *The Tempest*', www.rsc.org.uk/explore/ plays/tempest.htm. Aimed at students.

Suchet, David, 'Caliban', in *Players of Shakespeare 1*, ed. Philip Brockbank (1985). An actor's view.

Voss, Philip, 'Prospero', in *Players of Shakespeare* 5, ed. Robert Smallwood (2003). Another actor's view.

For a more detailed Shakespeare bibliography and selections from a wide range of critical accounts of the play, with linking commentary, visit the edition website, www.rscshakespeare.co.uk.

AVAILABLE ON DVD

The Tempest, directed by Percy Stow (1908), on *Silent Shakespeare* (DVD 2004). Twelve minutes of brilliant visual innovation: easily the best Shakespeare from the age of silent film.

The Tempest, directed by Derek Jarman (1979, DVD 2004). Highly original, punk-influenced, sometimes camp.

The BBC Shakespeare: The Tempest, directed by John Gorrie (1980). Staid, literalistic, not recommended.

Prospero's Books, directed by Peter Greenaway (1991, DVD 2007). Extraordinary re-visioning, in which John Gielgud as Prospero speaks all the lines; sometimes pretentious but dazzlingly inventive attempt to fuse the play's magic with the quasi-magical technological potential of cinematic art.

REFERENCES

1 E. K. Chambers, *William Shakespeare: A Study of Facts and Problems* (2 vols, 1930), Vol. 2, p. 342. The performance took place in the Banqueting House.
2 Chambers, *Shakespeare*, Vol. 2, p. 343.
3 *The Diary of Samuel Pepys*, ed. Robert Latham and William Mathews (1972), Vol. 8, pp. 521–2.
4 Alden T. Vaughan and Virginia Mason Vaughan, *Shakespeare's Caliban: A Cultural History* (1991), p. 180.
5 Vaughan and Vaughan, *Shakespeare's Caliban*, p. 181.
6 John Russell Brown, *Shakespeare's Plays in Performance* (1966), p. 109.
7 Vaughan and Vaughan, *Shakespeare's Caliban*, p. 183.
8 Lady Benson, *Mainly Players: Bensonian Memoirs* (1926), p. 179.
9 William Winter, *New York Daily Tribune*, 7 April 1897.
10 *Shakespeare's The Tempest as Arranged for the Stage by Herbert Beerbohm Tree* (1904), p. xi.
11 Beerbohm Tree, *Tempest*, p. 63.
12 Vaughan and Vaughan, *Shakespeare's Caliban*, p. 189.
13 Jeanne Addison Roberts, 'The Washington Summer Festival, 1970', *Shakespeare Quarterly*, 21 (1970), pp. 481–2.
14 Vaughan and Vaughan, *Shakespeare's Caliban*, p. 191.
15 Octave Mannoni, *Prospero and Caliban: The Psychology of Colonization* (1956), trans. from *Psychologie de la Colonisation* (1950).
16 Vaughan and Vaughan, *Shakespeare's Caliban*, p. 192.
17 Vaughan and Vaughan, *Shakespeare's Caliban*, p. 193.
18 David Hirst, *The Tempest: Text and Performance* (1984), p. 46.
19 Hirst, *Tempest*, p. 48.
20 Hirst, *Tempest*, p. 43.
21 Hirst, *Tempest*, p. 43.
22 Hirst, *Tempest*, p. 62.
23 Robert Brustein, Review of *The Tempest*, *New Republic* 213 (4 December 1995), pp. 27–8.
24 Ann Thompson, '"Miranda, Where's Your Sister?": Reading Shakespeare's *The Tempest*', in *Feminist Criticism: Theory and Practice*, ed. Susan Sellers (1991), p. 54.
25 Peter Brook, *The Empty Space* (1968), p. 135.
26 Christine Dymkowski, *The Tempest*, Shakespeare in Production (2000), p. 1.
27 KB, *Independent on Sunday*, 13 August 1906.
28 Bernard Levin, *Daily Mail*, 3 April 1963.
29 RSC Programme, 1963.
30 J. C. Trewin, *Peter Brook: A Biography* (1971), p. 135.
31 Michael Coveney, *Financial Times*, 13 August 1982.
32 Ned Chaillet, *The Times*, 13 August 1982.
33 *Cahiers Elisabéthains*, 22 (1982), p. 117.

34 Michael Billington, *Guardian*, 12 August 1982.
35 Alex Renton, *Independent*, 1 August 1988.
36 Kate Kellaway, *Observer*, 31 July 1988.
37 Michael Billington, *Guardian*, 29 July 1988.
38 Benedict Nightingale, *The Times*, 13 August 1993.
39 Russell Jackson, *Shakespeare Quarterly*, 45 (1994), p. 343.
40 Michael Billington, *Guardian*, 13 August 1993.
41 Alec McCowen, actor, interview with Peter Lewis, *Sunday Telegraph*, 8 August 1993.
42 Anthony Cookman on John Gielgud's performance, *Tatler*, 28 August 1957.
43 David Lindley, *The Tempest*, Shakespeare at Stratford (2003), p. 45.
44 Michael Billington, *Guardian*, 12 August 1982.
45 Billington, *Guardian*, 29 July 1988.
46 Dymkowski, *Tempest*, p. 24.
47 John Peter, *Sunday Times*, 31 July 1988.
48 Michael Coveney, *Financial Times*, 28 August 1988.
49 Michael Hordern, in *Shakespeare in Perspective*, Vol.1, ed. Roger Sales (1982), p. 174.
50 Judith Cook, *Shakespeare's Players* (1983), p. 167.
51 Francis King, *Sunday Telegraph*, 31 July 1988.
52 Helen Rose, *Time Out*, 3 August 1988.
53 Kellaway, *Observer*, 31 July 1988.
54 Jack Tinker, *Daily Mail*, 14 September 1982 (reviewing the London transfer).
55 Paul Vallely, *Mail on Sunday*, 18 September 1983 (London transfer).
56 Helen Rose, *Time Out*, 3 August 1988.
57 Christopher Hart, *Sunday Times* 13 August 2006.
58 Benedict Nightingale, *The Times*, 10 August 2006.
59 David Suchet, 'Caliban', in *Players of Shakespeare 1*, ed. Philip Brockbank (1985), p. 169.
60 Charles Spencer, *Daily Telegraph*, 2 March 1998.
61 Dymkowski, *Tempest*, p. 34.
62 Kate Kellaway, *Observer*, 15 August 1993.
63 Irving Wardle, *The Times*, 3 May 1978.
64 Suchet, *'Caliban'*, p. 172.
65 Cicely Berry, in *The Tempest*, RSC Education Pack, 1995.
66 Charles Lewsen, *The Times*, 24 October 1974.
67 Lindley, *Tempest*, p. 91.
68 Kate Bassett, *Independent on Sunday*, 12 May 2002.
69 Dymkowski, *Tempest*, p. 48.
70 RH, *Sunday Times*, 12 May 2002, p. 16.
71 Charles Spencer, *Daily Telegraph*, 9 May 2002.
72 Alec McCowen on 'Prospero and Ariel', *The Tempest*, RSC Education Pack, 1995, p. 23.
73 David Nathan, *Jewish Chronicle*, 20 August 1993.
74 Quoted in Trewin, *Peter Brook*, p. 135.
75 John Peter, *Sunday Times*, 15 August 1993.
76 Michael Billington, *Guardian*, 9 May 2002.
77 David Thacker, *The Tempest*, RSC Education Pack, 1995.
78 James McDonald, interview with Rex Gibson, *Times Educational Supplement*, 27 October 2000.

ACKNOWLEDGEMENTS AND PICTURE CREDITS

Preparation of 'The Tempest in Performance' was assisted by a generous grant from the CAPITAL Centre (Creativity and Performance in Teaching and Learning) of the University of Warwick, for research in the RSC archive at the Shakespeare Birthplace Trust. The Arts and Humanities Research Council (AHRC) funded a term's research leave that enabled Jonathan Bate to work on 'The Director's Cut'.

Picture research by Helen Robson and Jan Sewell. Grateful acknowledgement is made to the Shakespeare Birthplace Trust for assistance with picture research (special thanks to Helen Hargest) and reproduction fees.

Images of RSC productions are supplied by the Shakespeare Centre Library and Archive, Stratford-upon-Avon. This Library, maintained by the Shakespeare Birthplace Trust, holds the most important collection of Shakespeare material in the UK, including the Royal Shakespeare Company's official archives. It is open to the public free of charge.

For more information see www.shakespeare.org.uk.

1. Frank Benson as Caliban (1897) Reproduced by permission of the Shakespeare Birthplace Trust.
2. Alan Badel as Ariel (1951) Angus McBean © Royal Shakespeare Company.
3. Directed by Ron Daniels (1982) Joe Cocks Studio Collection © Shakespeare Birthplace Trust.
4. Directed by Sam Mendes (1993) Malcolm Davies © Shakespeare Birthplace Trust.

5. Directed by Peter Brook (1957) Angus McBean © Royal Shakespeare Company.
6. Directed by Michael Boyd (2002) Manuel Harlan © Royal Shakespeare Company.
7. Directed by Rupert Goold (2006) Manuel Harlan © Royal Shakespeare Company.
8. Bakary Sangaré as Ariel in *La Tempête* Directed by Peter Brook (1990) © Gilles Abegg.
9. Reconstructed Elizabethan Playhouse © Charcoalblue.

FROM THE ROYAL SHAKESPEARE COMPANY AND MACMILLAN